ALI
THE MOVIE AND THE MAN

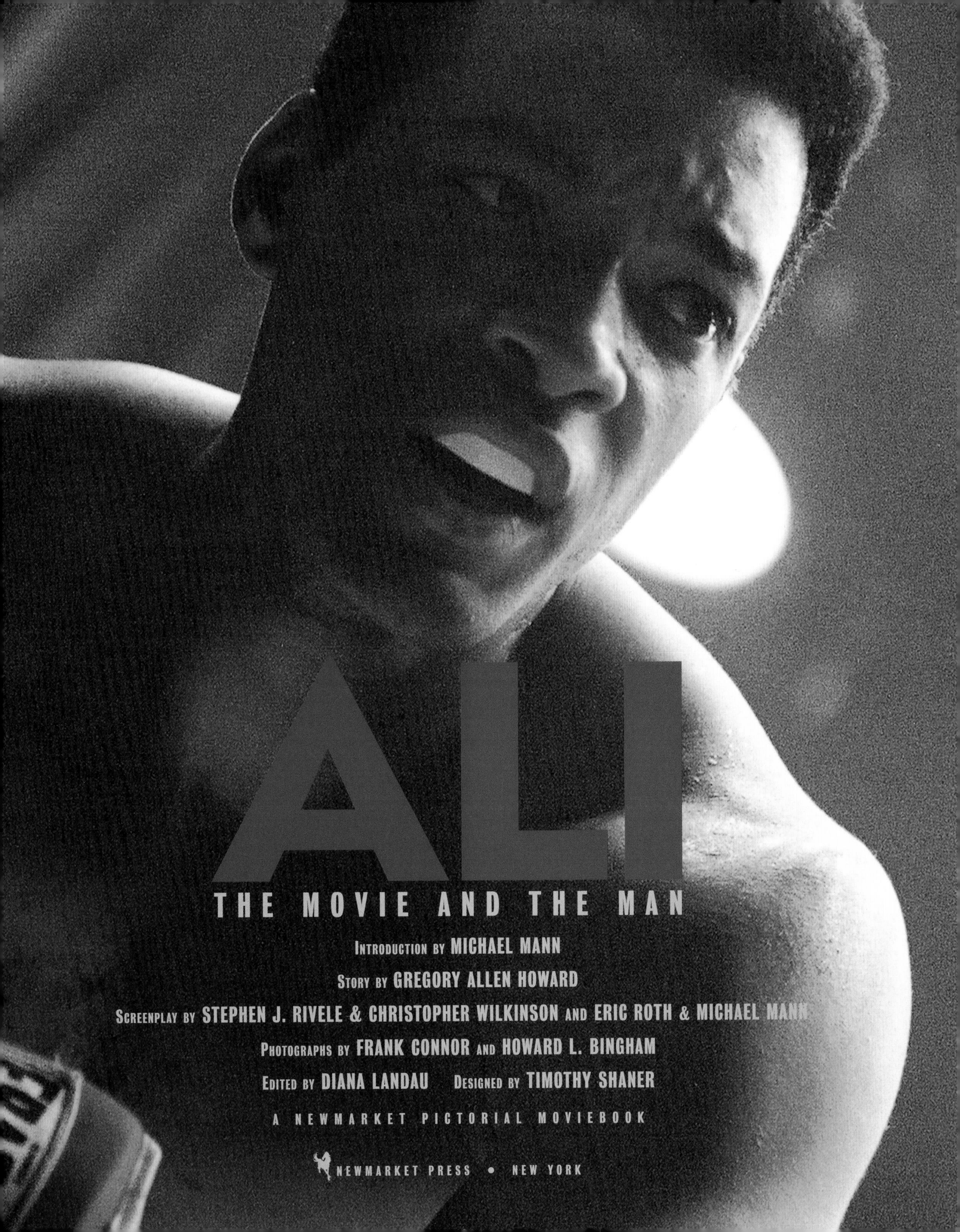

ALI
THE MOVIE AND THE MAN

INTRODUCTION BY MICHAEL MANN

STORY BY GREGORY ALLEN HOWARD

SCREENPLAY BY STEPHEN J. RIVELE & CHRISTOPHER WILKINSON AND ERIC ROTH & MICHAEL MANN

PHOTOGRAPHS BY FRANK CONNOR AND HOWARD L. BINGHAM

EDITED BY DIANA LANDAU   DESIGNED BY TIMOTHY SHANER

A NEWMARKET PICTORIAL MOVIEBOOK

NEWMARKET PRESS • NEW YORK

This book is published simultaneously in the
United States of America and in Canada.

First Edition

01 02 03 10 9 8 7 6 5 4 3 2 1

ISBN 1-55704-510-0 (paperback)
ISBN 1-55704-512-7 (hardcover)

Library of Congress Cataloguing-in-Publication Data is available on request.

QUANTITY PURCHASES
Companies, professional groups, clubs, and other organizations may qualify
for special terms when ordering quantities of this title. For information,
write Special Sales, Newmarket Press, 18 East 48th Street, New York,
NY 10017, call (212) 832-3575, fax (212) 832-3629,
or e-mail mailbox@newmarketpress.com.

www.newmarketpress.com

Manufactured in the United States of America

Other Newmarket Pictorial Moviebooks include:

Planet of the Apes: Re-imagined by Tim Burton
*Moulin Rouge: The Splendid Book That Charts
the Journey of Baz Luhrmann's Motion Picture*
The Art of The Matrix
Gladiator: The Making of the Ridley Scott Epic
Crouching Tiger, Hidden Dragon: A Portrait of the Ang Lee Film
*Titus: The Illustrated Screenplay, Adapted from
the Play by William Shakespeare*
*The Age of Innocence: A Portrait of the Film Based
on the Novel by Edith Wharton*
Cradle Will Rock: The Movie and the Moment
The Sense and Sensibility Screenplay and Diaries
Saving Private Ryan: The Men, the Mission, the Movie
Amistad: A Celebration of the Film by Steven Spielberg
Bram Stoker's Dracula: The Film and the Legend

Contents

Introduction
Becoming Ali

by Michael Mann

OPPOSITE: *Muhammad Ali contemplates his upcoming bout with Ernie Terrell at the weigh-in, Houston Astrodome, February 6, 1967. Photo Herb Scharfman/TimePix.*
ABOVE: *Director Michael Mann and Will Smith on the set.*

As Mike Marqusee claims in his book about Ali, *Redemption Song*, "the sixties [were] about the growth of a global consciousness [rising] from below. For people all over the world, Ali embodied that consciousness." Ali knew what it meant to be representative. What neighborhood he lived in, how he wore his hair mattered. It sent signals to white and black America. He was and is controversial and revered. And he drew strength from the masses cheering, "Ali, boma ye!" in Zaire in 1974. In this transaction . . . and in the ring against George Foreman, in Zaire it was as if a current passed from those masses of people, filling him with power and determination. . . .

Ali fulfilled a role as if he were a character in a story. But not a story someone's telling. Rather, it's a story he was living. He knew he personified racial pride and self-knowledge; sacrifice and defiance. Moreover, his life became a living story, testifying to all that, at the very least, struggle is possible.

When someone asked him, "Are you going to be the people's champion, like Joe Louis?" he responded, "Yeah, I'm gonna be the people's champion—but not like Joe Louis, exactly . . . ." He was referring to Joe's patriotism but he wasn't criticizing either Joe Louis or patriotism. His point was that he wouldn't be anybody's poster boy and have his representation manipulated as had been Joe's. (Louis contributed his World War II salary to the war movement and then got

"Ali fulfilled a role as if he were a character in a story. But not a story someone's telling. Rather, it's a story he was living. He knew he personified racial pride and self-knowledge; sacrifice and defiance. Moreover, his life became a living story, testifying to all that, at the very least, struggle is possible."

—MICHAEL MANN

prosecuted by the IRS for his failure to pay taxes upon it.)

What Ali meant was that he wasn't going to straighten his hair and move to a white suburb like other successful fighters. Following Malcolm X's dictum, he would be a proud "Afro-American." Ali lived "black is beautiful" before the phrase became a slogan for Stokely Carmichael and the Black Panther party. He was not going to acquiesce to the de facto apartheid of mid-century middle America. That is, he would not let it divide him internally into what W. E. B. DuBois called "double consciousness": one identity for the white American establishment and another for Louisville's west side and Chicago's south side. He would be one man with one voice . . . one presentation without hesitation, without wavering. And, it would be very funny. . . .

So, Ali's life is larger than life. Its scale is monumental. Will Smith and I prepared for a full year before we started shooting. Will brought commitment and courage, a positive spirit to the daunting prospect of becoming Ali. He "became" Ali to the point where he dreamed in Ali's speech patterns and regional inflections. Will transformed himself through a carefully designed curriculum that brought together trainers Angelo Dundee

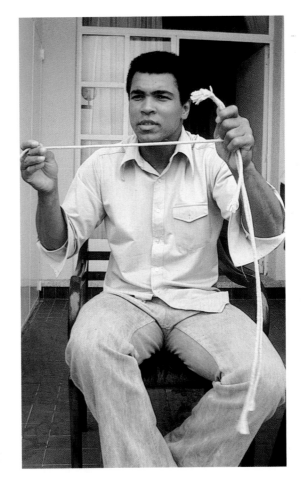

OPPOSITE: Will Smith trained as a boxer for over a year and added 35 pounds of muscle for the role of Ali. ABOVE: Ali performs magic. Zaire, 1974. Photo Howard L. Bingham.

"Will brought commitment and courage, a positive spirit to the daunting prospect of becoming Ali. He 'became' Ali to the point where he dreamed in Ali's speech patterns and regional inflections."

—MICHAEL MANN

and Darrell Foster, athletic neuro-programming and Islamic studies; former Black Panther Geronimo Pratt and Ali's first wife, Sonji Roi. We roamed Ali's neighborhoods in Chicago and Miami.

Most profoundly, Will became a boxer. The fighters he trained with pulled no punches, and Will became funny the way Ali is funny. Jeffrey Wright became photographer Howard Bingham, Ali's closest confidante. Ron Silver learned the trainer and cut man's trade from ever-youthful Angelo Dundee. Jon Voight so totally captured Howard Cosell that after four-and-a-half hours of prosthetics application, he would be Cosell all day long, both on and off camera. Jamie Foxx filled Drew "Bundini" Brown's triple roles of illiterate poet, shaman, and Falstaff. Angelo Dundee and Muhammad Ali showed up in our re-creation of Miami's Fifth Street Gym.

Only Will Smith has the balls, the intel-ligence, the charm, and the discipline to take on the role of Muhammad Ali. One morning, while Will put on gloves and sparred with Ali at our training facility in Santa Monica, I was in the ring with a video camera. I saw a look cross Will's eyes and thought, "He's not really going to do what I think he's going to do . . ." He did, and Will launched into "Man, I have russled with an alligator. I done tussled with a whale. Beat up lightning. Throw'd thunder in jail." Muhammad paused, turned to Dundee and Howard Bingham. . . . "Man, whyn't you tell me I was so crazy?"

ABOVE: Michael Mann and Will Smith go over notes on the director's breakdown sheet for a scene in Ali's Jeffrey Street apartment, Chicago. OPPOSITE: Ali with a broken jaw protects his face as Ken Norton throws another punch in his 12-round split decision win, April, 1973. Photo Bettman/Corbis.

Muhammad Ali, born Cassius Marcellus Clay, Jr., in Louisville, Kentucky, on January 17, 1942, got his first boxing lessons from an Irish-American cop named Joe Martin, who thought he was teaching a 12-year-old boy how to protect his bicycle from neighborhood bullies. But by age 16, Cassius had won the Louisville Golden Gloves tournament as a light heavyweight and advanced to the quarterfinals of the regional championship in Chicago.

After graduating from Louisville's Central High School in 1960, he won the National Golden Gloves competition and the Amateur Athletic Union title, capping the year with a gold medal at the Rome Olympics. But upon his return from Italy, with the medal literally around his neck, Clay was refused service in a Louisville diner. One story, since discounted, is that he chucked his medal into the Ohio River in anger at the slight; in any case, the medal was lost.

Sponsored by a consortium of white Louisville businessmen, Clay had his first professional fight on October 29, 1960, a six-round win by decision. Clay took his career development into his own hands at this stage by signing Angelo Dundee as his trainer. Under Dundee's tutelage, he rapidly developed his unique boxing style. In November 1962, Clay defeated 49-year-old Archie Moore to earn a shot at the heavyweight champion, Sonny Liston.

OPPOSITE: Ali training at Deer Lake, Pennsylvania, 1974. RIGHT: Ali and singer Sam Cooke, 1964. Photos Howard L. Bingham.

The young fighter also took charge of his own promotion, recording "I Am the Greatest" and boasting about his boxing, his beauty, and his poetry to anyone who would listen. On February 26, 1964, the day after defeating Liston to win the World Boxing Association championship, he shocked an already bemused public by declaring that he had converted to the religion of Islam. His acceptance of the teachings of Elijah Muhammad alienated many fans, black and white. But Ali remained unconcerned about those who would not accept the depth of his convictions—even the WBA, which refused to sanction his rematch with Liston, claiming he was fighting under a name other than the one on his boxing license.

In May 1964, Ali took his first trip to Africa, and within two months after his return, met and married Sonji Roi. They would divorce a little more than a year later because of Sonji's refusal to conform to Muslim customs.

In the following year, a controversy over Ali's first-round knockout of Liston during their rematch left the champ with a tainted crown. Ali spent most of the remainder of 1965 in exhibition matches but did fend off one title challenge from former champion Floyd Patterson, whom he knocked out in the 12th round.

In 1966, his contract with the Louisville busi-

nessmen having expired, his repute as a fighter quickly catching up to his boasts, and his stature as a leader in the black community growing, Muhammad Ali was reclassified 1-A by the Selective Service. He responded to Uncle Sam's calling in rhyme,

Keep asking me, no matter how long
On the war in Vietnam, I sing this song
I ain't got no quarrel with the Viet Cong.

Ali continued to make statements with his fists as well. He defended his title five times in 1966, the last against Cleveland Williams at the Houston Astrodome. In February 1967, he returned to Houston to defend his title against Ernest Terrell. But Terrell's taunts—particularly his repeated referral to the champ as "Cassius Clay"— got under the skin of Ali, who punished the challenger in what some writers called a cruel fight.

On April 28, 1967, Muhammad Ali officially refused induction into the U.S. Army, claiming conscientious objector status as "a minister of the religion of Islam." Ten days later, he was indicted by a federal grand jury in Houston for draft evasion. The all-white jury convicted him, and the judge imposed the maximum sentence of five years imprisonment and a $10,000 fine. His passport was revoked, and as a convicted felon, he was barred from fighting in the U.S., effectively ending his career.

But Ali's life was far from over. He continued studying and teaching the words of Elijah Muhammad and, on August 17, 1967, married 17-year-old Belinda Boyd. While he couldn't earn a living boxing, he turned to the college lecture circuit for money to feed and house his now growing family. He officially announced his retirement on February 3, 1970, while his appeal was still pending before the Supreme Court. On June 28, 1971, his conviction was overturned in a 8–0 decision—not based on any violation of civil liberties but because the FBI had conducted an illegal wiretap on Ali's phone.

He quickly arranged fights with Jerry Quarry and Oscar Bonavena and won both by knockouts.

ABOVE: Ali with Elijah Muhammad and Elijah's son, Herbert. Chicago, 1964. OPPOSITE: Ali getting his hands wrapped before a fight by Angelo Dundee. Photos Howard L. Bingham.

Then, in March 1971, Ali fought Joe Frazier for the WBA title that had been taken from him. The former champion lost in a 15-round decision at Madison Square Garden that sent both fighters to the hospital. Frazier didn't fight again for 10 months. Ali scheduled five three-round exhibition bouts over a period of two days in June, then beat Jimmy Ellis to win the North American Boxing Federation crown in July. He defended his NABF title five times until losing it to Ken Norton on March 31, 1973. Six months later he regained the title from Norton, and in January he beat Joe Frazier, again defending his NABF crown. The next challenge was wrestling the far more prestigious WBA title away from the imposing new champion, George Foreman.

The Ali-Foreman fight in Zaire earned Ali $5 million and the world heavyweight title that would be his for four more years, through 10 successful defenses. He would lose the crown in February 1978 to Leon Spinks, only to win it back from Spinks that September. Ali announced his retirement in 1979 but was tempted back into one last title fight—at the age of 39—against

Larry Holmes on October 2, 1980. The younger boxer pulverized him. Ali fought once more, losing a nontitle fight to the undistinguished Trevor Burbick in 1981 before hanging up the gloves for good.

In retirement, it was announced that he was suffering from Parkinson's Syndrome, which affected his motor skills, most noticeably his speech. It is generally presumed the disease was brought on by accumulated blows to the head during his career. But the ailment has not affected his mental faculties or his determination. In 1990, Ali went to Iraq to negotiate with Saddam Hussein for the release of hostages just prior to the Persian Gulf War. And in 1996, Ali's lighting of the Olympic torch in Atlanta became one of the most memorable moments in the history of the games.

Ali has done most of his legendary philanthropic works anonymously. He has donated millions of dollars to individuals and organizations without consideration for religion or race, including Jewish old-age homes, Catholic churches, and numerous colleges. Muhammad Ali was elected to the Boxing Hall of Fame on September 14, 1987.

The Cast

WILL SMITH as
Muhammad Ali

JAMIE FOXX as
Drew "Bundini" Brown

RON SILVER as
Angelo Dundee

JEFFREY WRIGHT as
Howard Bingham

JON VOIGHT as
Howard Cosell

MYKELTI WILLIAMSON as
Don King

JADA PINKETT-SMITH as
Sonji Clay

NONA GAYE as
Belinda Ali

MICHAEL MICHELE as
Veronica Porche

16

MARIO VAN PEEBLES as
Malcom X

GIANCARLO ESPOSITO as
Cassius Clay, Sr.

CANDY BROWN HOUSTON as
Odessa Clay

PAUL RODRIGUEZ as
Ferdie Pacheco

BARRY "SHABAKA" HENLEY as
Herbert Muhammad

CHARLES SHUFFORD as
George Foreman

MICHAEL BENTT as
Sonny Liston

JAMES TONEY as
Joe Frazier

AL COLE as
Ernie Terrell

und
1

"I am the greatest!"

1964...

The Gulf of Tonkin Resolution authorizes the use of U.S. military forces in Vietnam. . . The Free Speech Movement at University of California, Berkeley, signals the beginning of a decade of student protests. . . The Ku Klux Klan murders activists Goodman, Schwerner, and Chaney in Mississippi; two weeks later the Civil Rights Act is passed. . . The Beatles make their first triumphant tour of the United States. . . Twenty-three-year-old Cassius Marcellus Clay wins the Heavyweight Championship of boxing.

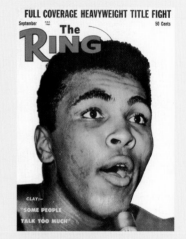

At the start of 1964, the talented young fighter known as Cassius Clay is in Miami, training for the defining bout of his career: a match with the feared Heavyweight Champion Sonny Liston. He has already won an Olympic gold medal and 19 professional fights. His photogenic face and form have already made him known to millions of Americans. And he has gained a reputation as a loudmouth, hailing his own invincibility in interviews and verse, even predicting the round in which his opponents would fall. Usually he is right. The press and public are trying to get a handle on this volatile young man, part of a rebellious generation and so different from the archetypes of black fighters they understand: compliant and patriotic men like Floyd Patterson or Joe Louis, or street thugs like Liston. What they don't know—yet—is that Clay has been attending meetings of the Nation of Islam under the mentoring of Malcolm X, an affiliation that would have a profound impact on his career, his image, and his soul.

As Cassius prepares to meet Liston, moving through the milieu of black Miami in the early '60s, we see in flashback some of the events that shaped him: his father's job as a sign painter in Louisville, the only work this talented artist could get; black people crowded in the back of a Louisville bus; searing photos of the lynching of Emmett Till; and a meeting of Clay's "owners" —a syndicate of white Louisville businessmen. We meet Cassius' supporters and cornermen: trainer Angelo Dundee, Drew "Bundini" Brown, Luis Sarria, Dr. Ferdie Pacheco, his brother Rudy; and we witness the skepticism of the press corps—Howard Cosell, Jimmy Cannon, and others—about Clay's chances as fight night nears. Liston predicts, "I might hurt that boy bad," and they believe it. We're there at the famous weigh-in, where Clay's behavior convinces Liston he's truly crazy, messing with his mind as Ali would do to so many others. And we're in the ring on February 25, 1964, for the momentous fight—in Clay's corner and inside his head. The camera shows us what it's like to be 23, to be Cassius Clay, to be on top of your game and to be about to own the world. "I am the greatest! I shook up the world!" he says.

After he does it, he fails to show up at any of the victory parties at the fancy hotels. He talks quietly with a few friends, plays with Malcolm's children, and falls asleep on a motel couch.

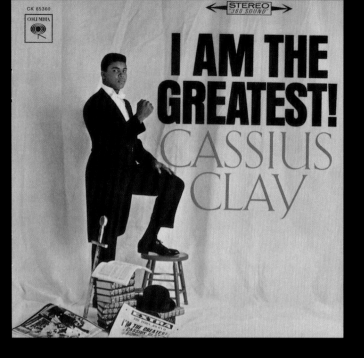

CK 65360

"I don't think it's bragging to say I'm something a little special."

— CASSIUS CLAY INTERVIEW IN
SPORTS ILLUSTRATED, FEBRUARY 24, 1964

This is the legend of Cassius Clay,
The most beautiful fighter in the world today.
He talks a great deal and brags indeedy
Of a muscular punch that's incredibly speedy.
This brash young boxer is something to see
And the heavyweight championship is his destiny.
He *is* the greatest!
This kid fights great, he's got speed and endurance;
But if you sign to fight him, increase your insurance.
This kid's got a left, this kid's got a right;
If he hits you once you'll sleep for the night.
And as you lie on the floor while the Ref counts ten
You pray that you won't have to fight me again.
The fistic world was dull and weary;
With a champ like Liston, things had to be dreary.
Then someone with color, someone with dash,
Brought fight fans a-running with cash—
CASSIUS CLAY!

— FROM *I AM THE GREATEST*, ALBUM RECORDED
BY ALI, RELEASED IN 1963

Clay the Contender

The buildup to the fight was a spectacle in itself. One day the Beatles, on their first American tour, visited Clay at his training gym. Although they had never met before, they all climbed into the ring and fell into a hilarious comedy routine that looked as though it had been rehearsed for days. John and Ringo and Paul and George fell down like dominoes and popped up like jacks-in-the-box as Cassius pretended to beat them up. Whether or not he could beat Liston, everyone agreed that Cassius was a championship clown.

— *NEW YORK TIMES* SPORTSWRITER ROBERT LIPSYTE

Remember, this was Miami, pre-civil rights and all that stuff, the Deep South, and Muhammad would run across the MacArthur Causeway to the gym, and I got calls from the police saying that there's some tall skinny black guy *running*—and did I know anything about it. I said that's our guy, Cassius Clay.

— TRAINER ANGELO DUNDEE

ABOVE: Will Smith as Cassius Clay, training in Miami for the first Liston fight, with Ron Silver (seated at desk) as Angelo Dundee. LEFT: Ali and the Beatles, Miami, 1964. Photo Howard L. Bingham.

Opposite: Ali trains with Sonny Liston ringside, Miami, 1963. Photo Howard L. Bingham. Top: Jamie Foxx as Drew "Bundini" Brown, Ron Silver as Angelo Dundee, and Lawrence Mason, far right, as Luis Sarria in the movie. Above: Michael Bentt as Sonny Liston.

The Liston people were sure of a knockout, and so, too, was the Louisville Sponsoring Group [Clay's financial backers]. "I have to be honest—until the last minute, I knew that Cassius couldn't possibly beat Sonny Liston, and when the time came to draw up contracts my entire orientation was that this was going to be his last fight," the group's lawyer, Gordon Davidson, said. "My only prayer was that Cassius wouldn't get hurt."

— David Remnick

The big thing for me was observing how Liston acted out of the ring. I read everything I could where he had been interviewed. I talked with people who had been around him, or had talked with him. I would lay in bed and put all of the things together and think about them, to try to get a good picture of how his mind worked. And that's how I first got the idea that if I would handle the thing right, I could use psychology on him—you know, needle him and work on his nerves so bad that I would have him beat before he ever got in the ring with me. And that's just what I did.

— Cassius Clay in Playboy, 1964

Louisville Boy

The story that my boxing career began because my bike was stolen is a true one. . . . I was twelve years old, and me and Johnny Willis, my closest buddy, had been out riding around on our bikes until the rain got too heavy. We were looking for something else to do when Johnny suddenly remembered seeing an ad for a black business exhibition at Columbia Auditorium on 4th and York. The auditorium is a big recreational center, with a boxing gym and a bowling alley. Every year the black people in the city hold a big bazaar, the Louisville Home Show, at the Columbia Gym.

At first I didn't want to go to the Home Show very much, but when we read the leaflet we saw that there would be free popcorn, free hot dogs and free candy. Besides, my father had bought me a new bike for Christmas, a Schwinn with red lights and chrome trim, a spotlight in the front, whitewall tires and chrome spokes and rims, and I wanted to show it off.

At the show we focused in on the food, and we hung around eating until seven o'clock, when everybody was leaving.

The rain was still coming down heavy as we left, so it took a while for us to notice that my bicycle was gone. Angry and frightened of what my father would do, we ran up and down the streets, asking about the bike. Someone told us to go downstairs to the Columbia Gym. "There's a policeman, Joe Elsby Martin, down there in the recreation center. Go and see him."

I ran downstairs, crying, but the sights and sounds and smell of the boxing gym excited me so much that I almost forgot about the bike.

There were about ten boxers in the gym, some hitting the speed bag, some in the ring, sparring, some jumping rope. I stood there, smelling the sweat and rubbing alcohol, and a feeling of awe came over me. One slim boy shadowboxing the ring was throwing punches almost too fast for my eyes to follow.

"You'll have to give me a report," Martin said calmly, and wrote down what I told him. Then, as

I was about to go, he tapped me on the shoulder. "By the way, we got boxing every night, Monday through Friday, from six to eight. Here's an application in case you want to join the gym."

I was about 112 pounds, skinny, and I'd never had on a pair of boxing gloves. I folded up the paper and stuck it in my pocket, thinking it was a poor thing to take home instead of a bike.

— MUHAMMAD ALI WITH RICHARD DURHAM,
THE GREATEST: MY OWN STORY

ABOVE: A composite photo of a young Cassius Clay and a young Will Smith.

Origins

The home into which Cassius Clay was born in 1942 wasn't privileged but neither was it desperately poor. His parents, Cassius, Sr., and Odessa, worked hard to help their two sons along in life, she cleaning houses and he painting signs and billboards. "Cash" was mostly a good family man, though he had some problems with alcohol and woman-chasing. Odessa, a devout Baptist, was recognized for her sweet and steadfast nature everywhere she went—and in later years, Ali's family had to deal with some of the trials as well as the benefits of being close to a celebrity. Cassius and his younger brother, Rudy, were extremely close as kids, Rudy following his brother first into boxing and later into the Nation of Islam.

"I raised them on the best street I could," recalls Cash, "3302 Grand Avenue in the west end of Louisville." Louisville was a segregated city then, and there were definitely parts of town where young Cassius and his brother knew they couldn't go. Surprisingly, the big, strong, athletic Cassius didn't get involved in sports much until he discovered boxing. Brother Rudy gave him early lessons in dodging blows: Cassius would instruct his Rudy to throw rocks at him and fluidly evade every throw.

The AAU and Golden Gloves champion, receives Kentucky's 'Amateur Athlete of 1959' plaque.

Even at eighteen, Clay was the most vivid, the most alive figure I'd ever met. It was like meeting a great actor or an electrifying statesman, some sort of figure that had a glow, an energy inside him, and you knew right away that you'd be hearing about him for years.

— SPORTSWRITER DICK SCHAAP

Through a veil I could perceive the forbidden city, the Louisville where white folks lived. It was the Louisville of the downtown hotels, the lower floors of the big movie houses, the high schools I read about in the daily newspapers, the restricted haunts I sometimes passed, like the white restaurants and country clubs, the other side of the windows in the banks, and, of course, the inner sanctums of offices where I could go only as a humble client or menial custodian. On my side of the veil everything was black: the homes, the people, the churches, the schools, the Negro park with Negro park police. . . . I knew that there were two Louisvilles and, in America, two Americas. I knew, also, which of the Americas was mine. I knew there were things I was not supposed to do, honors I was not supposed to seek, people to whom I was never supposed to speak, and even thoughts that I was never supposed to think. I was a Negro.

— BLYDEN JACKSON

LEFT: Various composites created for the film using archival images of Cassius Clay and Will Smith. ABOVE: Michael Mann directs Candy Brown Houston as Odessa Clay and Maestro Harrell as the young Cassius, in a scene on a Louisville bus.

When the boys got older, I took them with me on jobs; taught them how to paint pretty good. Before he started fighting, Muhammad could lay out a sign. Draw letters, do the spacing, mix the paint, and fill it in right. . . . I was an artist, not just a sign painter. I was born painting, and if it wasn't for the way things were then, a lot more people would have known what I could do.

— CASSIUS CLAY, SR.

"Ohhhhhh, he was a big baby," says his mother, Odessa. "So active. Into everything. Always running. Jabbering away even before he could talk. He had a knockout punch when he was six months old.

"See these front teeth of mine? We were lying in bed and he hit me so hard they pushed apart, and then the dentist had to pull 'em out."

His father, Cassius, Sr., recalls, "First words he said were 'Gee Gee.' He was trying to tell us he was going to win the Golden Gloves."

— ROBERT LIPSYTE

The truly marvelous stuff that happened to me with Ali was meeting his mother and father. There you saw the two component parts of Ali walking the earth in separate forms. The bombastic, fast-talking father, the complete egoist, and that lovely, sweet, warm, wonderful mom. And one of the interesting things about Ali when I met him was, he had not integrated the maternal and paternal sides of his personality. You would see Cassius Senior come out in those pugnacious, bellicose statements, and five minutes later you'd see his mother come out in some lovely sweet gesture or lyrical line. It was like a noninsane schizophrenia.

— *SPORTS ILLUSTRATED* REPORTER JACK OLSON,
ON MEETING ALI IN 1964

ABOVE: Sonji Clay, left, and Odessa Clay, Miami, 1965. LEFT: Rudy Clay, left, in the ring, 1964. OPPOSITE: Cassius Clay, Sr., Louisville, 1967. Photos Howard L. Bingham.

Playing an Icon:
Will Smith on Ali

After a brilliant career in movies, music, and television, superstar Will Smith takes on the role of a lifetime—Muhammad Ali.

Smith most recently starred with Matt Damon in Robert Redford's *Bagger Vance*, that performance earning him an NAACP Award for Best Actor. Previously he starred in the box office hit *Wild, Wild West;* the Tony Scott thriller *Enemy of the State;* and two of the all-time biggest blockbusters: *Independence Day* and *Men in Black*, for which he recorded the Grammy-winning theme song. Earlier Smith starred in the action hit *Bad Boys*, the Oscar-nominated *Six Degrees of Separation*, *Made in America*, and *Where the Day Takes You*. Currently he is filming the highly anticipated *Men in Black 2* for director Barry Sonnenfeld.

Beginning his career in music, he cut his first record as a high school senior and shortly thereafter teamed with his friend Jeff Townes to record several platinum and multiplatinum albums as DJ Jazzy Jeff and the Fresh Prince. Smith's first solo album, *Big Willie Style*, has sold eight million copies. His follow-up album, *Willennium*, featured the hit single "Will2K" and both went double platinum. On television, Smith can still be seen in syndicated reruns of the enormously successful sitcom *Fresh Prince of Bel Air*, created for him by Quincy Jones.

Smith speaks thoughtfully and passionately about his feelings of kinship with Ali, his experiences on the film and working with Michael Mann, and Ali's importance to our times.

On playing an icon:

"Muhammad Ali is one of the few people who is famous not only in the United States and all of the western countries, but also in Islamic countries that don't get our music videos or our sports. They don't really know Michael Jackson, or who Michael Jordan is, and others we think of as big celebrities. Muhammad Ali and Nelson Mandela are probably the two most famous people in the world.

"Team Ali [as Smith calls the film] is the life story of one of the greatest figures of the last century, and the little sacrifice that I had to make—to take a little pain in the ring to tell his story properly—is nothing like the sacrifices that he made for his people and for people around the world. So, it's almost cathartic to be able to get hit and take those shots and stand up and keep fighting.

"I felt like we had a lot in common. I understand his love of life. I understand his love of children. I understand his desire to have people, friends, around. I can relate to a lot of things that drive him. But I don't know if I will ever be able to achieve that kind of greatness in my life. Playing the role is really sweet. But knowing what he went through to become the greatest of all time, you know things had to taste a little bitter sometimes too."

On Muhammad Ali as a symbol for younger generations:

"Ali beat Liston in 1964, when I wasn't even born. So I really had to go back and learn about Muhammad Ali. I mean, I knew he was a fighter and he beat up a lot of guys and he talked a lot. But I also knew that he stood up against the Vietnam War. Kids who are twenty-one today have no real sense of that era, no real sense of the Civil Rights movement or the anti–Vietnam War movement. Still, somehow they associate Ali with all that. But they have no idea of the depth of suffering that went into forming that association.

"He found the simplicity in life. He said: 'I'm going to live by the word of my God to the best of my ability. And my God tells me I should not be killing people in Vietnam.' So, it's really kind of easy: you do what you have to do to me. Whatever I have to lose, that's OK because I've already established what my priority is. We look at him and say, 'Wow! He's so deep and so complex.' What he's about is actually real simple: if you believe something is wrong, don't do it. No matter what somebody promises you, no matter how somebody threatens you, no matter what the repercussions are, live—or die—by what you believe is right. It's a simple concept. But it's not easy.

"I think that Ali's life gives such a wonderful picture of what you can be. He showed that who you are is not about what's around you. It's about who you decide you want to be, and do you have what it takes to be that person. Are you willing to sacrifice, to work the way you need to work, and to fight the way you need to fight? His life illustrates the joy and the pain of being who you want to be, committing to your God and living the way you want to live—spiritually, emotionally, physically, sexually—and how liberating that can be."

On working with Michael Mann:

"Michael Mann defies the laws of physics: He actually can get blood from a stone. Michael is Jack Nicholson in *A Few Good Men:* You want him on that wall. You need him on that wall. And you sleep well in your bed at night knowing he's on that wall, doing everything he can to make the film better. He's a perfectionist. He's driven.

"Michael Mann in his brilliant insanity needed to change the actual building that was the Tiger Lounge [a Chicago location] back into the Tiger Lounge. It probably took me about six months of working with him to understand why he's so set on doing things with such a level of authenticity. Why try to actually shoot in Elijah Muhammad's house in Chicago? Because there's life in the walls that you can't even imagine. And as an actor, when you sit in the place where the

character actually sat, when you drive down the street the character actually drove down—there's something spiritual and emotional that puts you into that place. For Michael, every single detail needs to be identical or as close to the moment as exists on this planet right now. That's why we didn't shoot the Caribbean for Africa—we shot Africa for Africa—because then you have experiences like I had with the children that add layers to my performance, which would not have existed shooting anywhere else.

"But I love that drive. I love the challenge. I love doing 35 takes to just get that one that's magic. It's the idea that you might have achieved 99.3 of everything you ever dreamed about, but 99.3 is not 100 percent, so it's a failure. And I love applying myself to that concept."

On his hopes for the film::

"I know we've made a film that's going to go down in history. Muhammad Ali and his family were involved with this film, so we feel that we got inside the inner circle and captured the essence of the man. But it's scary when you take on a living icon, a man who means so much to so many people, and every aspect of his life has already been recorded. You've seen the fights. You've seen pictures with him with his wives,

tapes of him with his kids. You've seen the draft board. So how do you make a movie about things people have already seen, or think they've seen? We had to attempt to find the truth of the man— something you don't really see when you watch him on television.

"So the film doesn't necessarily focus on the big events. They happen, but most of the story takes place with his friends: like in the hotel room after he decided he wasn't going to step forward at the draft board. The night he met his first wife. You see the rise and fall, not through the headlines but through the eyes of his friends and through his own eyes, as he sits in the gas station in Chicago, watching the '68 Olympics. You're seeing more of those personal moments—on top of the most amazing boxing footage ever committed to film.

"I feel like there's been a real purity about this experience, that people are just excited about the potential of being part of the Muhammad Ali film. It's not about money or the prestige, just a love of the man and a love for what we've delivered. Even the people whose neighborhoods we're taking over to shoot in—you know, a movie can be difficult to live with, 'cause it's your neighborhood and now people are saying you can't walk here or you've got to go around the back. But everyone is so receptive and excited. And that's what I'm connecting with. Just being here has recharged me."

In Cassius' Corner

Ali was fortunate to have one of the most outstanding "corners" ever to work in the fight game. Most of these men joined the young Cassius Clay early, before the first Liston bout, and stayed together as a team for years, while other supporters and hangers-on came and went. Their leader was Angelo Dundee, a veteran trainer who won respect from everyone around Ali, including his Nation of Islam associates, who distrusted most whites. Dundee, writes Thomas Hauser, "was clear as to his own role. He was a trainer. Getting Ali ready to fight was his job. He didn't involve himself in Ali's religious, political or social activities. . . . The only demand Dundee made was, when the bell rang, he was the boss. During a fight, when he gave orders, the other cornermen were expected to obey. The formula worked; it lasted for twenty years."

Dr. Ferdie Pacheco was the physician who attended all of Dundee's fighters, and he quickly became an indispensable member of the team. He may have saved the day at the weigh-in for the Liston fight, when the boxing commission's doctor threatened not to let Clay compete because his pulse rate had skyrocketed from the excitement; Pacheco assured everyone he could have Clay in condition to fight. He remained with Ali for more than two decades, then developed a successful private practice. Ali's exercise man and masseur was Luis Sarria, also hired by Dundee—"the greatest exercise man in the world" according to Pacheco.

But the most colorful cornerman surely was Drew "Bundini" Brown, an all-around caretaker and cheerleader to the champ. Flamboyant, alcoholic, and fond of white women, he had an up-and-down relationship with Ali but could motivate him like no one else. It was Bundini who came up with Ali's famous slogan, "Float like a butterfly, sting like a bee!"

ABOVE: Left to right, Ron Silver as Angelo Dundee, Paul Rodriguez as Dr. Ferdie Pacheco, Lawrence Mason as Luis Sarria, Jeffrey Wright as Howard L. Bingham, Jamie Foxx as Bundini Brown, at ringside. OPPOSITE: Ali with Bundini Brown, Miami, 1963. Photo Howard L. Bingham.

ABOVE: Ali's cornermen, left to right, Ron Silver (Angelo Dundee), Jeffrey Wright (Howard Bingham), Will Smith (Muhammad Ali), Paul Rodriguez (Ferdie Pacheco), and Jamie Foxx (Bundini Brown). They stand in the front yard of the house Cassius Clay rented in 1964 while training to fight Sonny Liston. BELOW: Muhammad Ali, on a visit to the Miami set, stands in the same yard. Photo Howard L. Bingham.

Ron Silver on Angelo Dundee

Philadelphia-born Angelo Dundee was among the most respected trainers in boxing even before his long and legendary association with Ali. He is portrayed in the film by stage and screen veteran Ron Silver, who had the advantage of Dundee's presence on the set as a consultant, advising him on every authentic detail down to how to tape a fighter's hands before a match.

Silver came to know his namesake well, and says: "Angelo is universally respected. He's one of the wisest men in the boxing business. What Angie always says is, you don't put something on Cassius. You can't be imperative with him or command him or say, do this, don't do that. It had to come to him his way. Ali had a very unorthodox style that Angie never really tried to change. He just tried to get him to enhance what he did.

"For example, after a day of sparring, he might

say, 'Hey, Daddy, look, the way you bend your left knee, when you did the left jab, for more power. It was terrific. I'm very impressed the way you bent your left knee.' And Ali would say okay, and go home. Of course, he had never bent his left knee the entire day. But the next day, when he went in, he was more conscious of it, and he would bend the left knee when he threw the left jab. That's how Angie would teach, if he had to teach. But basically it was just guiding Ali in what he did."

Silver most recently costarred in the features *Cutaway* and *Black & White*. On Broadway, Silver won a Tony Award for starring in David Mamet's *Speed-the-Plow*. He is also a former two-term president of Actors Equity Association. Among many other film appearances, he earned wide critical praise for his role as attorney Alan Dershowitz in *Reversal of Fortune* starring Jeremy Irons, and for his portrayal of Henry Kissinger in the TV movie-of-the-week *Kissinger and Nixon*.

LEFT: *Angelo Dundee instructs Ron Silver, who plays Dundee in the film, on the proper technique for wrapping a boxer's hands.*

A Fighter Who Can Act

"We started out with a motto," says Will Smith, only half-joking. "And that motto was: if making history was easy, then everyone would do it."

Smith's transformation—physically and psychologically—from 185-pound actor to 220-pound athlete went well beyond normal preparation for a movie role. And it began nearly a full year before cameras started rolling. Smith undertook a five-day-a-week, six-hour-day workout regimen composed of running in combat boots in the snow in the thin air of Aspen, Colorado; lifting weights; and taking shots to the ribs from experienced boxers. He began his weight training bench pressing 175 pounds; by the end of the year he was pumping 365 pounds of iron. But the toughest training was in the ring.

"Beyond looking like a fighter, my goal was to learn to think like a fighter," says Smith. "To do that I had to eat like a fighter, sleep like a fighter, assess situations in life like a fighter, and become a fighter. My trainer, Darrell Foster, said the only way for me to accomplish that was to lace up my gloves and when the bell rings, he was gonna bash my head in."

"Michael Mann's vision and Will Smith's vision was that this was not gonna be a movie where you're just faking the punches," says Foster, who for years worked with boxing great Sugar Ray Leonard, among others.

To enable Smith to effectively transform himself into Muhammad Ali, director Michael Mann developed a comprehensive training curriculum carried out by advisors from multiple disciplines.

Technically from a boxing point of view, Will is sound. He moves as well as any professional fighter I've seen, and he's dedicated his life for the last six months or longer to picking up all the nuances, all the mannerisms, all the things that are Muhammad Ali. He's really been able to elevate his skills, using months as years. But I think it starts with the spirit. And Will has really a warrior within. He looks fear right in the face and enjoys conquering it. He's got the heart of a champion.

— DARRELL FOSTER, WILL SMITH'S
PRINCIPAL FIGHT TRAINER

I always say Muhammad was great at what he did because gymnasium work wasn't drudgery for him. It was fun. Will Smith's got that approach with his whole profession, and he's embodied it in the way he trains. When he skips rope, you're looking at Muhammad, the rhythm. . . . You're all going to be pleasantly surprised what this kid can do.

— ANGELO DUNDEE, ALI'S TRAINER AND
TECHNICAL CONSULTANT ON THE FILM

One was Dr. James Puffer, Chair of Sports Medicine at UCLA and former head physician to the U.S. Olympic team. To help Smith hone his hand and eye reflexes, Dr. Puffer selected 11 of Ali's signature moves from the seminal Clay vs. Liston I fight. Each of these moves was recorded in a one-minute loop on videotape so that Smith could practice them over and over. He was a quick study, incorporating into his own technique such Ali trademarks as the shuffle and the feathery jabs intended to distract an opponent, setting him up for the jolt that really stings.

Another member of the training team who helped Smith refine the nuances of Ali's style was Michael Olajide, Jr., a one-time world middleweight contender. Olajide was struck by Smith's aptitude: "For Will to go from never boxing before to fully portraying Muhammad Ali is amazing. Ali's style is incredibly difficult to emulate. That Will can do it so well indicates his natural ability as an athlete and his professional ability as an actor."

Among the real fighters Smith would face in the movie were former cruiserweight champion Al Cole, former middleweight champ James Toney, former WBO heavyweight titleholder Michael Bentt, and current world-ranked heavyweight Charles Shufford.

Of Will Smith's boxing, Angelo Dundee declares, "If I'd have had him when he was 20, I could've made a champion out of him. He's got the physical skills and, more importantly, he's got the heart."

Smith had to use his boxing skills and acting ability to convincingly depict an entire decade of

Ali's life and career. "The hardest thing, I believe, was the acquisition of character," says Mann. "How do you think at 22 if you're Cassius Clay? And how is that going to be different from the way you think as Muhammad Ali at 32? How much can you tell about him by what he says? How much of what he says is guileless and how much is calculated to keep an opponent off balance—in or out of the ring?"

Smith studied and fought and trained and analyzed tapes and trained some more. He adhered to a strict diet, practiced his Louisville dialect with voice coach Denise Woods, and talked as much as possible with as many people as he could find who'd known Ali during those years. And he met with the Champ himself.

"The first time Will met Ali, Will started imitating him, right to his face," recalls executive producer Howard Bingham. "Will broke right into his Ali routine, jive-talking and all that. He was really good too. After a minute or so of watching Will do Ali, Ali turned to me and asked, 'Was I really that crazy?'"

Boxing is a hard thing to learn. It takes years and years. You never stop learning, and you've got a lot of different things to learn. Will has only been doing it for a year. That's nothing. But he's got his style down, and he can fight. Will is a good athlete. So he could become a really good fighter, if he kept doing it.
— WORLD-RANKED HEAVYWEIGHT CHARLES SHUFFORD, WHO PLAYS GEORGE FOREMAN

Will Smith started as an actor. Now he's a fighter who can act. . . . All the fighters here, myself included, we work with Will hard, and we have this saying in the gym: "Iron sharpens iron." So, you know, when you spar with guys of that caliber you have to improve. When we spar with Will, we try to put him through his paces. We try to take him on the journey Ali took.
— FORMER WBO HEAVYWEIGHT TITLEHOLDER MICHAEL BENTT, WHO PLAYS SONNY LISTON

"**R**ound eight to prove I'm great!" Clay shouted, holding up eight fingers. "Round eight!"

Liston smiled thinly and held up two fingers.

When it came time to weigh the fighters, Clay insisted that Bundini and [former heavyweight champion Sugar Ray] Robinson be allowed up on the platform. He refused to budge until the boxing commission officials bent their rules.

"This is my show, this is my show," he said.

"I'll keep him quiet," Bundini told the cops. "I have to be up there to keep him quiet." Finally, the commissioners relented and the police waved all three up. Clay weighed 210 pounds.

Then Liston stepped up on the scale.

"Liston, two hundred and eighteen pounds," shouted Morris Klein, the Miami Beach boxing commissioner. Liston stepped down from the scale.

"Hey, sucker!" Clay yelled up at him. "You're a chump! You been tricked, chump!"

Liston looked down at Clay with a slight, fatherly smile.

"Don't let anybody know," he said. "Don't tell the world."

"You're too ugly!" Clay shouted. "You are a bear! I'm going to whup you so baaad. You're a chump, a chump, a chump . . ." Clay's voice was shrill, his eyes were bugging out, and he was lunging around like a mental patient.

"No man could have seen Clay that morning at the weigh-in and believed that he could stay on his feet three minutes that night," Murray Kempton wrote later in *The New Republic*.

— DAVID REMNICK

I was there, and it looked to me like Cassius was having a seizure, all gathered up in his own hysteria, going on and on, totally out of control. It was hard to believe he could fight that night. Sugar Ray Robinson was trying to calm him down. There had to be six guys holding on to him, and it looked like he was struggling to throw all six around. Then, right in the middle of everything— and I don't know how many people saw this—he winked at Robinson. People were screaming and shoving and jockeying for better camera angles, and Cassius was probably having a ball.

— SPORTSWRITER MORT SHARNIK

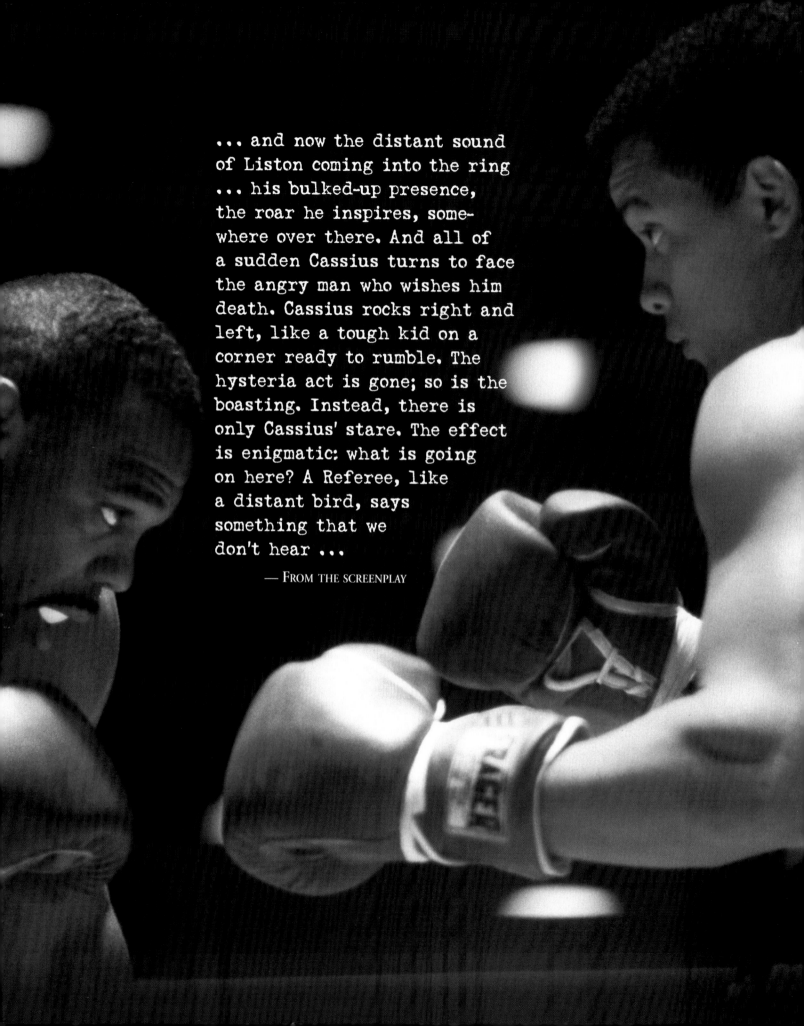

... and now the distant sound
of Liston coming into the ring
... his bulked-up presence,
the roar he inspires, somewhere over there. And all of
a sudden Cassius turns to face
the angry man who wishes him
death. Cassius rocks right and
left, like a tough kid on a
corner ready to rumble. The
hysteria act is gone; so is the
boasting. Instead, there is
only Cassius' stare. The effect
is enigmatic: what is going
on here? A Referee, like
a distant bird, says
something that we
don't hear ...

— FROM THE SCREENPLAY

When the opening bell finally sounded, near midnight, the shouting stopped and the fighting began. For the first two rounds Clay carried out his plan of dancing and dodging away from Liston's blows as the champion pursued him around the ring, surviving the few hard blows that landed. In the third round he went after Liston with rapid-fire combinations, opening a cut under his eye, and it slowly dawned on the spectators that the fight was starting to go his way.

Round Four began with more of the same—but then came the dramatic moments when Clay's eyes stung and watered—possibly from coagulant used on Liston's cuts—and he couldn't see. Between the fourth and fifth rounds, he told Dundee to cut the gloves off; he was done. But Dundee somehow got him back out there. "I only had a minute between rounds, and Barney Felix, the referee, was coming toward us to see what the problem was. Cassius was hollering, 'I can't see,' and I was scared they'd stop the fight. So I got his mouthpiece back in, stood him up, and said, 'This is the big one, daddy. Stay away from him. Run!'"

Midway through the fifth round, Clay's eyes cleared, and for the rest of the round, the two men fought on even terms. Round six belonged to the challenger. He hit Liston at will; Liston couldn't hit him. Just before the start of round seven, Howard Cosell (who was doing color commentary with Les Keiter's radio blow-by-blow) told his audience, "All I can say is, this is hard to figure out. Clay looked like he'd about had it—"

A roar from the crowd interrupted the thought, and then Cosell was screaming, "Wait a minute! Wait a minute! Sonny Liston is not coming out! Sonny Liston is not coming out! He's out! The winner and the new heavyweight champion of the world is Cassius Clay."

— THOMAS HAUSER AND ABC RADIO BROADCAST

It will go down in boxing history how the myth of Sonny Liston, The Great Unconquerable, was exploded in the flurry of the hammering fists of a brash, brave, and talkative young man.

Say all you will about Cassius and his great flow of language, his towering ego, his unorthodox manner of projecting himself. You must still admit that he put the deeds behind the words and came through victoriously.

Clay did more than win. He achieved the feat of outsmarting a man who had not only captured the title, but who had built a tremendous reputation for being able to scare his opponents, almost literally, to death.

Despite all those headlines about how worried Cassius was before fight time, the young Louisville Lip roared into the fray in the first round, attacking and proving that there was no fear in his heart.

Actually, Clay delivered a greater psychological beating to the now deposed champ than a physical one. His fight did not begin in the ring in Miami. It began months ago when Cassius initiated his psychological warfare, taunting Liston, making him angry and low-rating him.

I don't think there can really be any doubt or shadow cast upon Clay's clear-cut victory. Liston's failure to come out into the ring to take the rest of his beating is upheld by medical testimony.

However, most of us, who are accustomed to seeing the gladiators win their honors in the center of the ring and lose them there, could not help feeling a keen disappointment that Liston should go out like this. Frankly, I feel it was the beating he had taken and the cuts on his face which caused him to decide not to show for the next round.

— JACKIE ROBINSON, "CLAY EXPLODES LISTON MYTH," *CHICAGO DEFENDER*, MARCH 14–20, 1964

"I am the king! I
am the king! King
of the world! Eat
your words! Eat
your words!"

— ALI TO THE PRESS AFTER
HIS DEFEAT OF LISTON

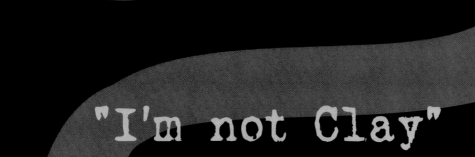

"I'm not Clay"

A change gonna come...

The boxing world, and everyone else, is stunned by Clay's victory over Liston. People still don't know what to make of this outspoken athlete who has lived up to his crazy boast. His good looks, talent, and spirit are appealing, and if he acts like the "right" kind of champion, he could become incredibly popular. But it's soon clear he's not going to fit white America's idea of who he should be. Just two days after the championship fight, he confirms his allegiance to the Nation of Islam, led by self-designated prophet Elijah Muhammad, and declares that he will no longer use the name his family inherited from Kentucky slaveowners: Clay. For the time being, he is "Cassius X." Escorted by Malcolm X, he tours Harlem to an ecstatic welcome. Malcolm confides that he's about to make a trip to Africa and urges Cassius to accompany him.

But a split has been widening between Malcolm and Elijah Muhammad, who suspends Malcolm's duties and bans him from contact with Cassius. Meanwhile, he summons the champion to his home and bestows a new name on him: Muhammad ("one worthy of praise") Ali ("most high"). Ali's new identity is sealed, and to keep him safely within the fold Elijah assigns his son Herbert to be his business advisor and spiritual guide. From then on the Muslims are deeply involved in Ali's career—which doesn't sit well with Ali's father, Cassius, Sr. In late 1964, Ali visits Africa after all, but with a group of Muslims led by Herbert. Landing in Ghana, Ali is overwhelmed to encounter a society where black people rule: are airline pilots, bankers, hotel managers. But when he crosses paths with Malcolm during the journey, he keeps his distance. He's made his choice.

Back in the U.S.A., as Ali trains for a rematch with Sonny Liston, a major distraction enters his life in the form of gorgeous, sexy Sonji Roi. Herbert Muhammad introduces her to the champ for a little R&R, but Ali falls hard and insists they marry. Although Herbert objects and Sonji wants no part of the demure Muslim women's dress code, he gets his way. As Ali's ties with the NOI grow stronger, he sinks lower in public opinion. A storm of bad press engulfs them when Malcolm X is assassinated while addressing a meeting in Harlem; the furor forces the Ali–Liston bout to be moved from Boston to a small arena in Maine.

The fight itself is controversial—Ali drops Liston with a hard right "barely a minute into the first round!" as Howard Cosell calls it—and many still doubt Ali's status as champ. And though his passion for Sonji still burns, she won't be a docile Muslim wife. Ten months into the marriage, he files for divorce.

Citizen of Islam

I met Ali—I think it was in March of 1961—when I was selling *Muhammad Speaks* newspapers on the street [in Miami]. He saw me, said "Hello, brother," and started talking. And I said, "Hey, you're into the teaching." He told me, "Well, I ain't been in the temple, but I know what you're talking about." And then he introduced himself. He said, "I'm Cassius Clay. I'm gonna be the next heavyweight champion of the world." I said, "I know you, man. I followed you in the Olympics." Then he asked, "Do you want to come around and look at my scrapbook?" so I went to his hotel room. He was sharing it with another fighter. The scrapbook was full of articles about himself, and I looked at it real good. He was interested in himself, and he was interested in Islam, and we talked about both at the same time. He was familiar in passing with some of our teachings, although he'd never studied or been taught. And I saw the cockiness in him. I knew if I could put the truth in him, he'd be great, so I invited him to our next meeting at the mosque.

— ABDUL RAHAMAN, FORMERLY KNOWN AS SAM SAXON OR CAPTAIN SAM, ALI'S FIRST DIRECT CONTACT WITH THE NOI

Islam is a religion and there are 750 million people all over the world who believe in it, and I'm one of them. I ain't no Christian. I can't be when I see all the colored people fighting for forced integration get blowed up. They get hit by stones and chewed by dogs, and they blow up a Negro church and don't find the killers. I get telephone calls every day. They want me to carry signs. They want me to picket. They tell me it would be a wonderful thing if I married a white woman because this would be good for brotherhood. I don't want to be blown up. I don't want to be washed down sewers. I just want to be happy with my own kind.... A rooster crows only when it sees the light. Put him in the dark and he'll never crow. I have seen the light and I am crowing.

— ALI AT A PRESS CONFERENCE, FEBRUARY 27, 1964

When Muhammad Ali joined the Nation [of Islam] it was a continuation of what we knew was happening already. Everybody had seen Malcolm [X] down in his camp. Everyone knew that he was teaching him, instructing him at that particular time, so when he changed his name, we said very simply, "That's his name." In fact, when people called him Cassius Clay, we would say, "That's not his name. Call the brother by his name. His name is Muhammad Ali. Go on, do it. Get it. Walk on." And we were very pleased and very happy.

— SONIA SANCHEZ, POET AND MEMBER OF THE CONGRESS OF RACIAL EQUALITY (CORE)

If Negroes ever turn to the Black Muslim movement, in any numbers, it will not be because of Cassius or even Malcolm X. It will be because white America has refused to recognize the responsible leadership of the Negro people and to grant to us the same rights that any other citizen enjoys in this land.

— JACKIE ROBINSON, "CLAY EXPLODES LISTON MYTH"

OPPOSITE: Ali with Elijah Muhammad, New York, 1964. Photo Howard L. Bingham.

Malcolm, the Mentor

My first impression of Malcolm X was how could a black man talk about the government and white people and act so bold, and not be shot at? How could he say these things? Only God must be protecting him. He was so radical at that time, and yet he walked with no bodyguard, fearless. That really attracted me. What also attracted me, he says, "Why we called Negroes? Chinese are named after China. Cubans are named after Cuba, Russians after Russia, Germans after Germany. All people are named after their country. What country is called Negro?" I said, "Man, so true."

Malcolm said, "We don't have names." Weinstein, you know is a Jew. Here come Lumumba, Africa. Here come Chang Chow, a Chinaman. Here come Red Cloud, Indian. Here come Jim Washington. He could be black or white. We all got the slave names. We don't have our names. They named us in slavery. So I got me a name from Elijah Muhammad. Muhammad Ali.

— MUHAMMAD ALI

My father's relationship with Cassius Clay was not as a recruiter for the Nation so much as it was one individual meeting another and saying, "Why don't you join me in this organization so you can have direction and a family of supporters." It was more than counseling; it was a friendship. My father was an excellent big brother to many, and when he met Cassius, he saw greatness and wanted to offer a focus of motivation. My father loved Cassius like a brother, but once you were brought into the Nation, you became an entity of the Nation. Your allegiance was to the organization before it was to any individual except, perhaps in the eyes of some, to Elijah Muhammad.

— ATTALLAH SHABAZZ, DAUGHTER OF MALCOLM X

From the moment of their first meeting, Malcolm and Clay formed a special bond. "I liked him," Malcolm wrote. "Some contagious

OPPOSITE TOP: Malcolm X and Ali, Harlem, New York, 1964. Photo Howard L. Bingham.

quality about him made him one of the very few people I ever invited into my home. Our children were crazy about him." For the next two years, Clay would arrange his itinerary so he could come see Malcolm speak as often as possible. After the sermon, the two would spend hours discussing the Koran. Malcolm carefully nurtured his new protégé in the ways of the Nation.

— HOWARD BINGHAM AND MAX WALLACE,
MUHAMMAD ALI'S GREATEST FIGHT

Not many people know the quality of the mind he's got in there. He fools them. One forgets that though a clown never imitates a wise man, the wise man can imitate the clown.

— MALCOLM X ON ALI

I recall principally the adoration between Malcolm and Muhammad Ali. I remember Malcolm's great pride whenever he would talk of . . . "My younger brother." Malcolm saw Ali as someone who had real capability to be a messenger in America and tell young black people what was going on. It wasn't important to him that Ali take sides in his differences with Elijah Muhammad. He simply wanted Ali to be free and strong.

— ALEX HALEY

Mario on Malcolm

Malcolm X is played in the film by Mario Van Peebles, who most recently starred in the independent films *Raw Nerve* and *Blowback*. He earned an NAACP Image Award for his role in Clint Eastwood's *Heartbreak Ridge*. The son of groundbreaking African-American filmmaker Melvin Van Peebles, he made his own mark in independent cinema as director and star of the hit film *New Jack City*, followed by directing and starring turns in the multicultural western *Posse* and the political drama *Panther*. He has also co-starred in the features *Highlander III, Jaws: The Revenge, Gunmen, Los Locos,* and *Solo.* On television, Van Peebles most recently starred in the Showtime series *Rude Awakening* and the network tele-feature *The Sally Hemmings Story.* He also starred in the title role of *Emperor Jones* for PBS and in the A&E presentation *Third & Oak: The Pool Hall,* for which he earned a Cable Ace Award nomination.

> "Ali and Malcolm were two men who didn't pull punches. And this script doesn't pull punches."
>
> — ACTOR MARIO VAN PEEBLES

Van Peebles shares his unique perspective on the champ, Malcolm, and the making of *Ali:*

"Muhammad Ali changed the status of black people in America," explains Van Peebles. "America's a tricky place. If you say 'by peaceful means,' like Martin Luther King did, or if you say 'by any means necessary,' like Malcolm X did, they shoot you both. They'll give one guy a holiday but they'll shoot you both.

"Muhammad Ali galvanized people in a different way—not just in America but internationally when he stood up against the draft, when he took on his Muslim name and religion and when he spoke out against his own government. When he went broader and started to travel, Malcolm said to him, 'You're an international troublemaker now.' Of course, he meant that as a reminder that the whole world was now watching what he did and listening to what he said.

"If you look at a lot of things that young Cassius was saying when he was preparing to fight Sonny Liston, you can see Malcolm there. Malcolm urged Cassius to look at Christianity, or the way Christianity has been misused or misrepresented, where European men were oppressing people of color. And he showed Cassius a picture of Sonny Liston with a white clergyman. He was saying, you see where Liston is going for spiritual guidance. He's going to the white man, the sons of folks that owned people like you and me. Whereas you're coming to the natural religion—which he believed for the black man was Islam. And so Cassius came in with a whole different energy, way beyond that of a typical fighter—seeing the fight in almost a religious sense, as if it was fate that he would take on this mantle.

"And when Cassius later on says, I'm not

LEFT: Re-creating history: Michael Mann stages the scene in which Malcolm X and Martin Luther King, Jr., played by LeVar Burton, meet for the first time, using a historical photograph for reference.

going to go fight in Vietnam. Why should I? when right here in America I can't get my constitutional rights? A lot of that thinking is his way of articulating what he got from Malcolm, I think.

"Ali and Malcolm were two men who didn't pull punches. And this script doesn't pull punches. When my father and I were taking the script for *Panther* around to the studios ten years ago, guys would say, "Oh, we love it, man. It's great." And then tell us they'd have to make the Bobby Seale or Huey Newton character white to get a white audience in the theater. Or make up a white girl who teaches the young future Panthers how to read. Ideas like that. The way you'd have a movie about Indians but it had to star Kevin Costner, or about Biko but starring the white guy who interviewed him, or about the Civil Rights movement but focusing on two white FBI agents, or about

heavyweight champs who they know look like Tyson or Ali but are played by Stallone. So categorically people of color were reduced to sort of exotic backdrop.

"But since then, Spike Lee did *Malcolm X* and I did *New Jack City* and Singleton did *Boyz N the Hood.* And now it's gotten to a new level where a brother like Will Smith has raised the ante and can be directed by Michael Mann in the Ali film, and not have it be from the perspective of the white guy interviewing Ali, but from Ali's perspective. And not shy away from the relationship with Malcolm and the things Malcolm said and impressed upon Ali, and embrace that as the way it was—not saying we have to whitewash it to make it a success.

"So just in the time that I've been in cinema, I've seen that change. And it's really interesting and exciting to be a part of that dynamic."

Discovering Africa

In May [1964], Ali left for a month-long tour of Egypt, Nigeria, and Ghana with his close friend the photographer Howard Bingham and two friends from the Nation of Islam, Osman Karriem (formerly Archie Robinson) and Herbert Muhammad (the third of Elijah's six sons and Ali's future manager). In the years to come, the emotion of the trip to Africa—the demonstrations of affection, the chants of "Ali! Ali!" in the remotest villages—would all be repeated many times and in many countries. But this trip was the first of its kind, and Ali was thrilled. It thrilled him to be among Africans, "my true people," as he put it; it thrilled him to meet such world leaders as Kwame Nkrumah; and it thrilled him to be recognized in places that would never have known, or cared about, Joe Louis, much less Rocky Marciano. This was, in short, his first taste of what it would be like to be Muhammad Ali, international symbol, a fighter bigger than the heavyweight championship, the most famous person in the world. This was the start of it, the start of Ali's transfiguration.

— DAVID REMNICK

By coincidence, during the course of Ali's African trip, the boxer arrived in Ghana—through which Malcolm X was passing on his way to Mecca. At one point, the two passed each other in a marketplace, but didn't speak. Moments later, Ali turned to Herbert Muhammad—the Messenger's son who was travelling with him—and offered an assessment of his former teacher.

"Man, did you get a look at him? Dressed in that funny white robe and wearing a beard and walking with a cane that looked like a prophet's stick? Man, he's gone so far out he's out completely. Doesn't that just go to show that Elijah is the most powerful; nobody listens to that Malcolm anymore." This conversation was captured in an FBI surveillance report.

Ali sounds like a man trying to convince him-self he had done the right thing in choosing the Messenger over Malcolm. In later years, he would feel shame about turning his back on the man who had advanced his spiritual growth, guided his thinking, and been like family to him.

— HOWARD BINGHAM

It was in Africa that he became something he hadn't been before. We were driving down a road in Ghana. Usually, there was nobody on the roads. Outside of the capital, it was just towns forty miles apart with nothing in between. One day, we got in the car with no plan, and five minutes after we started driving, there was like a beating of drums. Then people started showing up on the road.

"Ali! Ali!"

I'd never seen anything like it before. I was sitting there with this kid, and people were coming out of nowhere, lining the road, calling "Ali! Ali!" I saw this kid sitting there. He didn't say anything. It's like he was hypnotized. Do you have any idea what it must have been like for him to see thousands of people materialize out of nowhere and know they were there just for him? That day I saw the birth of a new human being. It was like Cassius Clay came to an end and Muhammad Ali emerged.

— OSMAN KARRIEM (FORMERLY ARCHIE ROBINSON),
AN EARLY NOI ASSOCIATE OF ALI'S WHO
ARRANGED THE TRIP TO AFRICA

OPPOSITE INSET: Ali's first visit to Africa, 1964. Photo Howard L. Bingham.

Stand by Me

Howard Bingham holds a unique place in the life of Muhammad Ali and in the making of *Ali*. He met the soon-to-be-champ in 1962, while a photographer for a small Los Angeles newspaper, and struck up a friendship by offering Cassius and his brother Rudy, just arrived in L.A., a tour around town. And for the 39 years since, they've been as nearly inseparable as two extremely busy men can be. Amid all the boxing staff, business advisors, spiritual counselors, and hangers-on, he has simply been the true friend Ali most needed, ready to speak out if asked (and sometimes if not), to lighten a tense moment with his sly wit, and to give quiet, steadfast support in times of need.

His photos of the Champ are among the most indelible images in the public's awareness of Ali's life and athletic career. Hailed for his consummate skill with subjects, Bingham has photographed personalities from Elvis to Malcolm X and documented events from the Detroit riots to the election of Nelson Mandela. His subjects have ranged from presidents and monarchs to the proud residents of Mound Bayou, Mississippi, where he lived while photographing one of America's poorest communi-

> "If Ali was Don Quixote, then Bingham was his Sancho Panza."
> — THOMAS HAUSER

ties for a *Life* magazine essay. He has been named Photographer of the Year by the Kodak Corporation and is a winner of the American Society of Photographers International Award. Among his many freelance assignments, Bingham has served as a unit photographer on several movie sets for his friend Bill Cosby, who brought him into the cameramen's union by hiring him to work on his television show in 1969. Bingham even found time to make a run for Congress in 1978 in his home district in California.

Howard Bingham's name appears twice on the credits for *Ali:* as executive producer and naturally as a character in the film, played by actor

ABOVE: Howard Bingham and Ali in a car, Las Vegas, 1965. Photo Lee Balterman/TimePix. OPPOSITE: Jeffery Wright as Howard Bingham.

"I'll tell you straight out: With
everything I went through with Ali,
the one person I could always
count on was Howard Bingham."

— BELINDA ALI, ALI'S SECOND WIFE

Jeffrey Wright. Bingham worked for 11 years to bring Ali to the screen, developing the story with several writers and at last finding the ideal "corner" in the partnership of Columbia Pictures and Michael Mann. His lifetime of companionship with Ali was invaluable in retracing Ali's steps for the film; he was with the shoot from day one, consulting on locations and events, even helping re-stage specific images using his own still photographs as reference.

While the crew was filming in Chicago, in Ali's old Southside neighborhood, Bingham and a couple of cast and crew members went to see if they could get a peek at Ali's former home. Bingham knew the owners who had purchased the place from Ali, who were happy to show the visitors around inside.

Bingham also arranged for Ali to visit the film set several times. He remains a frequent traveling companion of the Champ, helping him and his wife, Lonnie, navigate the huge crowds that gather everywhere he goes.

And of course Bingham worked closely with Jeffrey Wright on the actor's portrayal of him and the friendship. "There's nothing that will be seen in this film that Howard hasn't seen in life," Wright observes. "And that is an incredible journey when you're with someone like Muhammad Ali. For me, as a kid, Ali was our poet warrior, fighting against institutions and establishments designed to crush black people. He represented the intelligent warrior."

What was it like to embody a character like Bingham, who was so central to the story and also constantly around on the set? Wright says, "In some ways it's easy because you have a guy there who has a take on every scene that we're doing. You know Howard stutters, and words don't come as easily to him readily and as smoothly as images through the lens. So his most eloquent voice is his camera lens—and he showed me his beautiful photographs chronicling this story, which helped tremendously. But then I have to speak like Howard," he laughs. "And that's when he's tempted to throw things and curse at me and run me off the set. But we get through it. He's just such a wonderful guy to be around."

Tongue firmly in cheek, Wright adds, "Actually I think I'm alive now because Howard Bingham knows me. 'Cause he seems to know everyone living. I don't know what I was before, but now that Howard Bingham knows me, I'm living."

Jeffrey Wright recently starred as Martin Luther King in the HBO production *Boycott*. From saint to sinner, he costarred in 2000 as a New York drug dealer in *Shaft*. Wright made his big screen debut in the title role of *Basquiat*, the true story of the graffiti artist who became one of America's most controversial painters of the 1980s, following this with a starring role in Ang Lee's *Ride with the Devil*.

On stage, Wright recently earned high praise for his portrayal of Marc Antony in the Shakespeare in the Park production of *Julius Caesar*. He won a Tony Award for his work in *Angels in America*. He also completed a long, successful run on Broadway in the award-winning celebration of African-American music and history *Bring in da Noise, Bring in da Funk*.

OPPOSITE INSET: Howard Bingham and Muhammad Ali, 1993. Photo Gordon Parks.

In the loose, rambling hours between hostilities, Muhammad Ali was constantly in search of someone he could open his soul to. Crowds were welcome. He loved crowds, but even more he loved to plant himself dead center in a bunch of school kids, sound off, then warm to their glee and adoration. Yet there were also times when despair crept in and refused to leave him, when suddenly there was just loneliness. During those rare moments he had a need to attach himself to someone who would leave him with his silence. No one in his entourage was more suitable for that than Howard Bingham.

. . . Howard's words and photographs recall so many things about Muhammad Ali—things of different sizes falling restlessly upon my memory. Only a rare few have as many selves as Ali. To know and really understand him one has to sink deeply in the geography of his soul. Howard has done that while observing him with the sensitivity of a blind man.

— PHOTOJOURNALIST GORDON PARKS

Everybody says I love people, so it's only fair that I have the best friend in the world, and that's Howard Bingham. He never asks for anything; he's always there when someone needs him. There's no one like him. He's the best there is. And if you write that, I don't want Howard to think I'm getting too soft, so write down that he's lucky I'm his friend too. And tell him I said I'm the only person in the world who likes him.

— MUHAMMAD ALI

Road Work:
Re-creating Ali's America

During the course of filming over 90 days in four states and three countries, the company utilized a prodigious 127 sets. Wherever possible, Michael Mann tried to film in the places that had a real-life connection to Muhammad Ali.

Among the first of these were the Sports Arena and Olympic Auditorium in Los Angeles. Ali fought at the Sports Arena in 1962, first against Alejandro Lavorante, later against one of his idols, Archie Moore, winning both times. He only attended bouts at the Olympic, but that venue has its place in history as Los Angeles's most famous fight arena, bringing local and national TV audiences the Friday Night Fights, "live from the Olympic Auditorium" weekly during the 1950s and 1960s.

The company moved to Mann's hometown of Chicago in the dead of winter, where filming took place mainly around Ali's old neighborhood on Chicago's Southside. As a filmmaker, Mann was familiar with the Windy City, having shot *Thief*, parts of *Manhunter*, and the television series *Crime Story* there. Among the locations for *Ali* were the house where Elijah Muhammad once lived, next door to the current residence of Louis Farrakhan.

On another chilly evening, the production took over five blocks along 79th Street to film a sequence in which Ali passes the landmarks of his old neighborhood. Mann chose this major thoroughfare because Ali used to walk it when he lived nearby in the 1970s. Fans young and old lined the sidewalks to watch the filming, which lasted well into the night. While the younger onlookers were there to catch a glimpse of Mann guiding Smith through the scene, many older bystanders enjoyed a stroll down memory lane, remembering when they saw the Champ pass these storefronts.

"I probably haven't seen a Sinclair Gas station since Ali moved out of the neighborhood," one man commented. "I remember when he and his pals used to hang out there." In fact, Ali's "hangout" was a garage several blocks away (since torn down), countered Bingham, who spent many a leisurely day with him there. But memories of a legend create an alternate reality, no less true to the people remembering than if they'd actually happened.

Another building with special significance for Ali was the Tiger Lounge, where he and Bingham used to go dancing and where Ali had his first date with his first wife, Sonji. Here the filmmakers had to do some major urban archeology and restoration before filming the scene with Will Smith and Jada Pinkett-Smith swinging and swaying in the footsteps of their real-life counterparts. They took away furniture, put up walls, and shot right on the site where Ali's first romance had blossomed—adding a hot group of girl singers in place of the jukebox that used to supply the music.

After moving to New York for a few scenes of Ali walking the streets of Harlem with Malcolm X, the company relocated to Miami, where Ali lived while training for the first Sonny Liston fight. In Miami, one of the shooting locations was the backyard of the house Ali once rented in the Overtown district. Ali paid one of his occasional

visits to the set while the crew was filming in Miami, much to the delight of the neighbors.

Another of the landmark locations in Miami was the Fifth Street Gym, owned by Angelo Dundee's brother, where the young contender Cassius Clay trained for his first championship fight. "The Fifth Street Gym was an integral piece of our story but, unfortunately, it had been torn down about fifteen years ago," says production designer John Myhre. "But Angelo Dundee, who was an advisor on the movie, still lived in Miami and he helped us scout for another building. When we found one, he went through it with us, saying, 'Yeah, this one smells right. This one could be it. This'll work.' He also gave us some guidance as to how the real gym was set up.

"I've worked on historical films before but usually the people have been dead for a few hun-dred years," notes Myhre, an Oscar nominee for his work on *Elizabeth*. "But on this, with people like Angelo and Howard Bingham around, we could, and so often did, pick up the phone to ask 'What color was that car?' or 'Which side was the driveway on that house?' For the gym, Angelo was able to tell us, 'Oh, no, the ring wouldn't be there, it would be over here' and 'I didn't have a big fancy desk, just a little one over in that corner.' And that really helped."

ABOVE: The Sports Arena in Los Angeles stands in for the Houston Astrodome during the filming of Ali's bout with Ernie Terrell (played by Al Cole, right). BELOW: Photo montage of a Chicago street, decorated by the Ali production team to look as it would have in the 1960s. (Some of the parked cars are the wrong vintage; these do not appear on film.)

The Tiger Lounge in Chicago was the perfect example of how Michael likes to use real locations to get a feel for the history there. The Tiger Lounge was once the place to be in Chicago. When Ali would come into town, that's where his friends were and that's where he would go dancing.

Unfortunately, when we got there, we found out the lounge had been closed for 20 years. It had been turned into a furniture store. Most of the ceiling had been torn away and several of the walls ripped out. But there was still a section of the store that had these beautiful, curvy soffits and lighted inset glass pieces and this wonderful broken mirror whose pieces they'd put over a wavy wall. Of course, we said, "Fabulous, we can re-create this on a soundstage." But Michael said, "We won't re-create it, we'll restore it."
— PRODUCTION DESIGNER JOHN MYHRE

OPPOSITE: Will Smith as Ali on a wintry Chicago street during his exile. ABOVE: David Elliott as Ali's friend, the soul singer Sam Cooke, whose music is featured in the film. RIGHT: The Fifth Street Gym set in Miami.

"Yeah, this smells right."
— ANGELO DUNDEE, WHILE SCOUTING A MIAMI BUILDING TO SERVE AS THE FIFTH STREET GYM SET

Sonji:
Scent of a Woman

His marriage to Sonji Roi, described as a Chicago barmaid, was surprising and seemed uncharacteristic. She was five years older than he, divorced, a mother, a non-Muslim, a glamorous and worldly woman. Ali had often fantasized about the beautiful natural girl he would find in a backwood cabin, court with songs and gentle play, and after she fell in love with his soul, reveal "WHO I REALLY AM," and whisk her off to share his throne. Now, suddenly clumsy and callow, he walked five steps ahead of a siren with flashing thigh. Once, during an impromptu press conference at poolside, Sonji appeared above us, on the balcony in front of their motel room. "Ah-leeeee," she crooned.

"What is it?" he snapped, glancing up from the corner of his eye. "What you want?"

"You, Ahhhh-leeeeeee. Now."

Sheepishly mumbling apologies, he rose and left.

— ROBERT LIPSYTE, *NEW YORK TIMES MAGAZINE*, MARCH 7, 1971

When Ali was traveling in Egypt in the spring of 1964, [Herbert] Muhammad watched with amusement as the new champion fell in love with yet another pretty waitress. "I got a girl in the States who's better-looking than she is," Muhammad told him. Before leaving for Africa, Muhammad had taken a few pictures of [Sonji] Roi at his photograph studio. He had a copy of one of the photographs in his briefcase and showed it to Ali. The champion was impressed and hoped Herbert would introduce him to Roi when they got home.

— DAVID REMNICK

When Sonji and I split, I just about went crazy, sitting in my room, smelling her perfume, looking at the walls. But it was something that had to happen. She wouldn't do what she was supposed to. She wore lipstick; she went into bars; she dressed in clothes that were revealing and didn't look right.... One time, I slapped her. It was wrong. It's the only time I did something like that, and after I slapped her I felt sorrier than she did. It hurt me more than it hurt her. I was young, twenty-two years old, and she was doing things against my religion, but that's no excuse. A man should never hit a woman.

— MUHAMMAD ALI

ABOVE: Ali and Sonji at Disney World, 1965. Photo Howard L. Bingham.

He asked me to marry him that night [July 3, 1964, their first date]. I didn't know if he was serious or not. I didn't know anything about him. But I was alone in the world. I didn't have a mother to go home and ask. I had to make the decision myself. After we spent some time together, I felt needed by him. He was strong, but he didn't know a lot of things. He needed a friend, and what better person than me?

— SONJI ROI

Ali vs. Liston II

Ali's rematch with Sonny Liston originally was scheduled for November 16, 1964. But just three days before the date, the champion became acutely ill in his Boston hotel room and was rushed to a hospital, where he underwent surgery for a severe hernia. The fight had to be postponed for six months, and the older Liston "fought his heart out in training" and went stale during the delay, according to Norman Mailer, while Ali continued to get stronger.

Meanwhile, the growing flap about his ties with the Nation of Islam led Massachusetts authorities to refuse to host the rescheduled fight—especially after Malcolm X was assassinated in February 1965. Finally, the fight was moved to a small arena at a youth center in Lewiston, Maine. As the May date approached, an ugly rumor spread that Ali was going to be killed in revenge for Malcolm's death.

But fight night brought no such drama—just a swift and shattering end to the hopes of all who wanted to see Ali brought down. Just midway into the first round:

"He hit him so quick the cameras couldn't take it. He hit him with a shot Liston couldn't see. They're the ones that knock you out."

— ANGELO DUNDEE

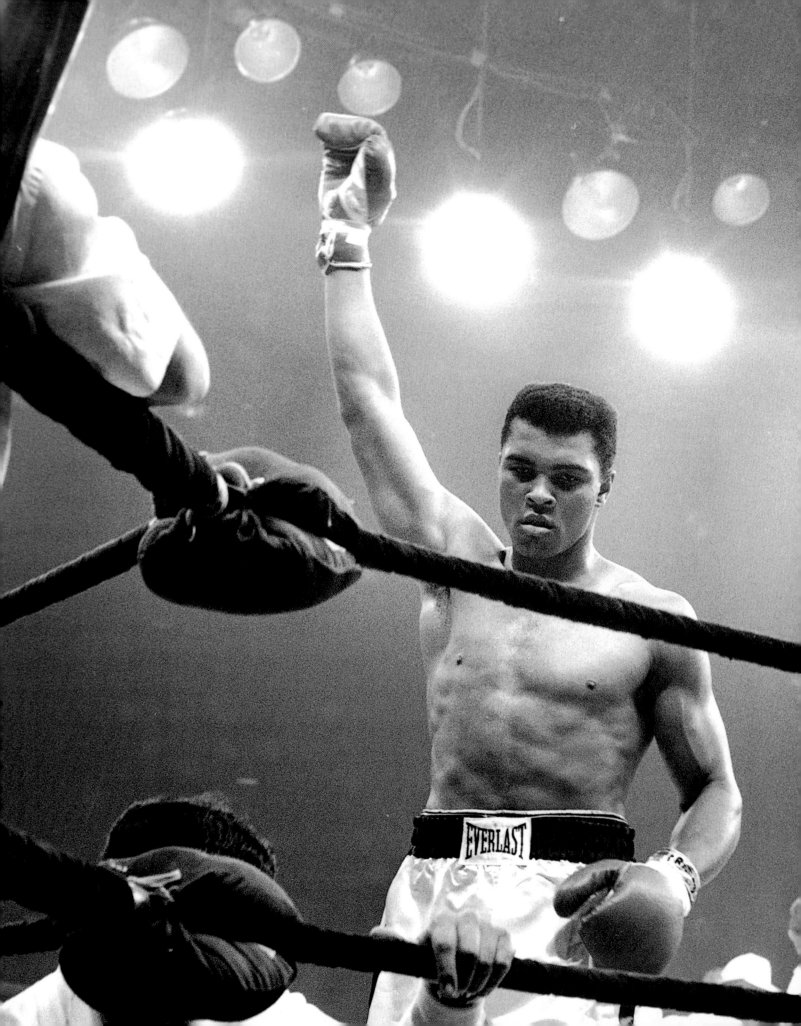

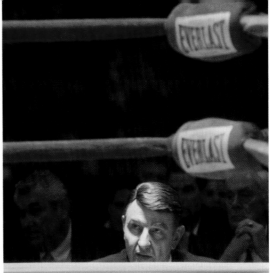

Then comes the moment that would bewilder so many in the arena. With Ali skimming along the ropes, Liston lunges forward with a left. Ali yanks back his chin just enough to avoid any damage, and then, as he pivots forward, throws a short, chopping overhand right to Liston's temple. Liston's head snaps to the side and he goes straight down to the canvas. It is possible that later in the fight, the punch might not have been enough on its own to floor Liston, but Liston is off-balance from missing the jab, frustrated, and, since it is still just a minute into the fight, cold. . . .

"That shot shivered Liston," Chicky Ferrara said at the time. Ferrara was an experienced trainer whom Dundee had placed near Liston's corner to discourage a repeat of the blinding incident in the last fight. "He blinked his eyes three times, like he was trying to clear his head, and I looked at Willie Reddish. I could see Reddish looked sick because he knew his fighter was in trouble."

Liston went down and rolled to his back, his arms stretched over his head. The rules of the game demand that the upright fighter retreat immediately before the referee starts his count, but Ali would not retreat. [Referee] Jersey Joe Walcott was too deferential. He didn't force Ali away but should have.

Instead, Ali stood directly above Liston. He kept his right hand cocked and started shouting down at Liston:

"Get up and fight, you bum! You're supposed to be so bad! Nobody will believe this!"

— DAVID REMNICK

RIGHT: Ali's victory over Sonny Liston, Lewiston, Maine, 1965. Photo Howard L. Bingham. ABOVE: Jon Voight as Howard Cosell, ringside at the fight.

und

3

"What's my name!"

Ain't got no quarrel...

A month before his second fight with Liston, Ali takes a qualifying exam for the U.S. military and receives a failing score on the mental aptitude test. He is embarrassed when the results are made public, but at least he's safe from the draft and can get on with his career.

Which he does, defending his title six more times in 1965 and 1966 while maturing into perhaps the best all-around professional fighter the world has seen. If he's not quite at the peak of his physical skills now, he is surely nearing it. But a different kind of fight looms. Early in 1966, the Selective Service abruptly reclassifies Ali as 1-A for the draft—following a policy shift that lowers the qualifying test score to gather in more young men for Lyndon Johnson's war in Vietnam. As Ali gets the bad news, the press descends to get his reaction, and after an exasperating few hours of questions, Ali gives them the headline they want: "Man, I ain't got no quarrel with them Vietcong."

Mainstream America unleashes its fury at his "unpatriotic" stance; his upcoming bout with former sparring partner Ernie Terrell is banned from Illinois and moved to Houston. Terrell, refusing to call Ali by his right name, earns a savage pounding in return—but the net around Ali is tightening. His claim as a conscientious objector is denied and he is ordered to report for induction. On April 28, 1967, again in Houston, his quick feet remain still when he's ordered to step forward; shortly thereafter he is convicted of refusing induction, stripped of his title, and forbidden to travel outside the U.S., making it impossible to fight abroad.

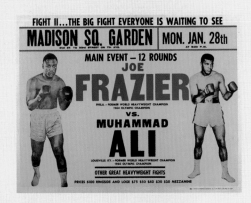

Ali's exile lasts three-and-a-half years, mostly in Chicago; it brings dark times. With no money to be made from boxing, the Nation of Islam edges away. Bundini Brown loses himself in New York and alcohol. The nation divides deeply over Vietnam; the '68 Olympics, black power salutes, the killing of Martin Luther King, Chicago's Days of Rage, come and go. There are bright spots: Bingham is always there, and Belinda Boyd, a young worker in a Muslim bakery, wins Ali's heart and starts a family for them. Broadcaster Howard Cosell gives him a voice in the media. Slowly his career comes back into view: the new champion, Joe Frazier, agrees to fight, and Ali reunites his entourage for an intense period of training. And at long last, in June 1971, the Supreme Court overturns his conviction—he's free again to fight anyone, anywhere.

Whether he will ever regain his crown is in doubt, though. Just a month earlier, Ali's incredible comeback has run headlong into the merciless fists of Smokin' Joe Frazier.

Champion Under Siege

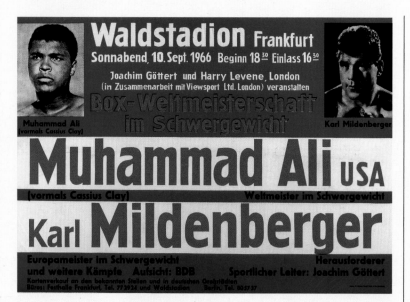

The first challenger for Ali's title was Floyd Patterson. A former champ himself, he had lost badly to Liston twice and was on the downhill slope of his career, but was eager to fight Ali to "reclaim the title for America," he said. "The Black Muslim influence must be removed from boxing," he claimed amid other attacks, to which Ali retaliated with his own verbal fireworks. But Ali spoke loudest in the ring, battering Patterson for 12 rounds yet never finishing him off—deliberately, most onlookers agree. Even one of his supporters, reporter Robert Lipsyte, compared the torture to "a little boy pulling the wings off a butterfly piecemeal."

His next fight was scheduled to be against Chicago's Ernie Terrell, who held the World Boxing Association title—but after the public uproar about Ali's Vietcong remark, the Illinois fight commission canceled the bout, and the only place the promoters could find to hold it was Toronto. Terrell backed out at that point, and instead Ali fought and beat the tough Canadian champ, George Chuvalo—amid calls for fight fans to boycott Ali's matches entirely.

It seemed impossible to arrange an Ali fight anywhere in the U.S., and his backers saw no other option but to have him fight overseas. Three bouts in Europe followed, against England's Henry Cooper and Brian London, and Germany's Karl Mildenberger. Not only did Ali triumph each time (the fight against Cooper was one of the bloodiest ever seen), but this sojourn abroad did much to confirm his status as the true world's champion. Prior to this, nearly all heavyweight championship fights since 1915 had taken place in the United States. The Mildenberger fight also was the first sports telecast ever to be transmitted by satellite.

Ali finished out 1966 in his own country, with a devastating win over Cleveland Williams at the Houston Astrodome, ending with a knockout in the third round—a match that to Howard Cosell marks "the greatest Ali ever was as a fighter."

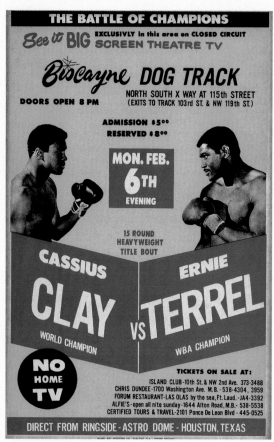

OPPOSITE: Ali hammers Patterson, 1965. Photo Corbis/Bettmann.

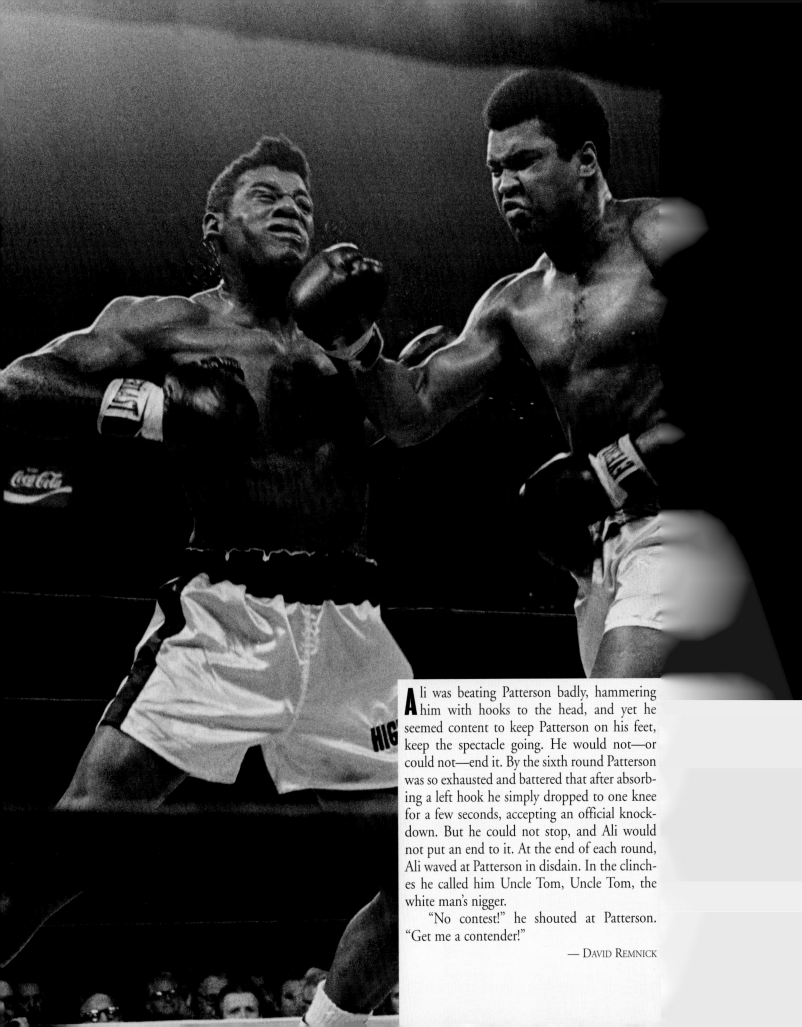

Ali was beating Patterson badly, hammering him with hooks to the head, and yet he seemed content to keep Patterson on his feet, keep the spectacle going. He would not—or could not—end it. By the sixth round Patterson was so exhausted and battered that after absorbing a left hook he simply dropped to one knee for a few seconds, accepting an official knockdown. But he could not stop, and Ali would not put an end to it. At the end of each round, Ali waved at Patterson in disdain. In the clinches he called him Uncle Tom, Uncle Tom, the white man's nigger.

"No contest!" he shouted at Patterson. "Get me a contender!"

— DAVID REMNICK

"If you couldn't write about Ali, you couldn't write. He made us all look good."

— ASSOCIATED PRESS SPORTSWRITER ED SCHUYLER

Ali and the Press

The athlete of the decade has to be Cassius Clay, who is now Muhammad Ali. He is all that the sixties were. It is as though he were created to represent them. In him is the trouble and the wildness and the hysterical gladness and the nonsense and the rebellion and the conflicts of race and the yearning for bizarre religions and the cult of the put-on and the changed values that altered the world and the feeling about Vietnam in the generation that ridicules what their parents cherish.

— REPORTER JIMMY CANNON

He was, of course, friendly to Black correspondents—indeed, interviewing Muhammad was often their apprenticeship. With no other famous Black man were they likely to receive as much courtesy: Ali answered questions in full. He answered them to microphones for future radio programs and to microphones for reporters with tape recorders, he slowed up his speech for journalists taking notes, and was relaxed if one did not take a note.

— NORMAN MAILER, *THE FIGHT*

Typically, his TV appearances were lighthearted. On the *Tonight Show,* he unveiled a poem he had written that has been acknowledged by the Guinness Book of World's Records as the shortest in history—"Whee! Me!" But the famous conservative intellectual William F. Buckley, Jr., well known for his debating skills, was anxious to challenge Ali's views on race and booked him on his weekly TV show for a more serious discussion. In a memorable exchange that proved Ali could hold his own against any opponent, in or out of the ring, Buckley fired the first salvo: "You have said that the white man is your enemy. Well, I happen to know this is not true. I believe you have been poisoned by your leader."

Ali jumped right in. "How can you say Elijah Muhammad is poisoning us to believe the white people are our enemy? It's you who taught us that you're our enemy. It was white people who bumped off Martin Luther King, it was white people who bumped off Medgar Evers, it was white people who bumped off Adam Clayton Powell. We didn't imagine this."

Buckley has rarely, if ever, publicly admitted being wrong. More inconceivable still would be an admission that he was bested by a mere athlete. But after the debate he told an interviewer, "I started out thinking he was simply special-pleading on his own behalf, but I ended up thinking he was absolutely correct."

— HOWARD BINGHAM AND MAX WALLACE

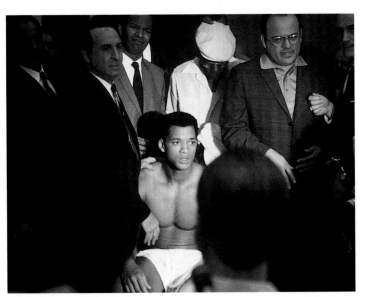

"You surprise me, Muhammad. . ."

Ali had a complicated relationship with the media. All of its members recognized him from the start as the best source of copy anywhere on the sports beat, and well beyond. From there they tended to split into camps: the old-line, traditional boxing writers disliked his style both in and out of the ring, loathing his Muslim ties and defiance of the draft. Younger sportswriters like Robert Lipsyte saw him as the dynamic new hope of a corrupt sport; black intellectuals like LeRoi Jones as the only black athlete able to articulate the righteous anger of black America in the '60s. And a whole fraternity of social commentators, from Norman Mailer to George Plimpton to Wilfred Sheed, seized on Ali as the perfect symbol for their turbulent times, and chronicled his fortunes in book after book.

But the journalist most identified with Ali is ABC sportscaster Howard Cosell, famed for his absurd toupee, stentorian voice, sharp insight, and a delivery almost as colorful as Ali's. The sports interview was just becoming a major feature of television when both men came on the scene, and Cosell would become its first great practitioner—largely due to his frequent, unpredictable, and hugely entertaining exchanges with Ali. Though they couldn't have been more different, the two genuinely liked and respected each other. Ali loved upending Cosell's dignity and appreciated his fairmindedness. Cosell often took Ali to task but truly admired his talent and his courage. For a long time he was the only major media figure to use the name "Muhammad Ali" in his broadcasts, and he vigorously defended Ali in his draft conviction case.

Cosell is portrayed in *Ali* by one of the film world's most versatile actors, Jon Voight. The Vietnam War, which had such impact on Ali's career, also profoundly shaped that of Voight, whose memorable performance as a paraplegic veteran in *Coming Home* won him an Oscar for Best Actor. Voight first met Ali in person in 1968, just after appearing in the classic *Midnight Cowboy*, which brought his first Academy Award nomination, and they stayed in touch from time to time.

"I called his house before the Zaire fight,"

ABOVE: Howard Cosell interviews Ali after his induction indictment, 1967. Photo Howard L. Bingham. OPPOSITE ABOVE: Muhammad Ali (Will Smith) and Howard Cosell (Jon Voight) in one of their memorable exchanges.

recalls Voight. "I really didn't intend to even mention the fight but it was on my mind just like it was on everybody else's, so the first thing out of my mouth was 'Well, what's gonna happen in the fight?' He almost never paused and thought about an answer but this time he did. He said, 'Well, I have to win, don't I?' He knew what he was carrying for everybody. He knew for himself he had to win his title back but just as much he knew what it meant to so many of us."

Voight's respect for the man was both personal and political—which was also true of the relationship between Ali and Howard Cosell. Given their collective prominence in the sports world, it's likely, Voight believes, that Ali and Cosell's friendship played a powerful role in the fight against bigotry during the explosive '60s and early '70s. "Howard was a fellow who backed Ali and took a lot of heat because of it," explains Voight. "When he came forth and called Muhammad Ali by his Muslim name, he received thousands of letters, most of them vilifying him with racial slurs. He had attacks from bigots probably all his life as a result of his public support for Ali. But he stood his ground."

Voight, like others, observes that there was a special chemistry between Ali and Cosell that made each more watchable than they would have been alone. "I do think that Ali will always be defined in some way by that relationship. Both of them had a gift for performing, self-promotion, and real entertainment. Also, Cosell was a lawyer, so his interviews were interrogative; they had that edge to them. And I think that that's what Cosell provided for Ali. For his part, Ali had the ability to play with people, and he was a natural tease. They were terrific together—no question about it."

Voight was recently featured in *Pearl Harbor* and *Lara Croft: Tomb Raider* (starring his daughter Angelina Jolie) and has recently starred in *A Dog of Flanders, Enemy of the State* (with Will Smith), and *Varsity Blues*. Among his other recent films are *The General, Mission Impossible*, Francis Ford Coppola's *The Rainmaker*, and Michael Mann's *Heat*.

Muhammad Ali is a figure transcendental to sport. He's important to the history of this country because his entire life is an index to the bigotry lodged deep within the wellspring of this nation and its people. . . . And Ali had the advantage of coming in the 1960s. . . . That time period was incredible, and Ali understood it; he was at the heart of it; he helped shape it all.

— HOWARD COSELL

"Man, I ain't got no quarrel
with them Viet Cong."

Lacking Due Process

OPPOSITE: *Ali the day he was indicted for refusing induction into the armed forces, 1967. BELOW: Ali with supporters of his decision: (front row) Bill Russell, Ali, Jim Brown, and Lew Alcindor; (back row, left to right) Cleveland Mayor Carl Stokes, Walter Beach, Bobby Mitchell, Lorenzo Ashley, Sidney Williams, Curtis McClinton, Willie Davis, Jim Shorter, and John Wooten. Cleveland, 1967. Photos Howard L. Bingham.*

It is in the light of my consciousness as a Muslim minister and my own personal convictions that I take my stand in rejecting the call to be inducted in the armed services. I do so with the full realization of its implications and possible consequences. I have searched my conscience and I find I cannot be true to my belief in my religion by accepting such a call.

My decision is a private and individual one and I realize that this is a most crucial decision. In taking it I am dependent solely on Allah as the final judge of these actions brought upon by my own conscience.

I strongly object to the fact that so many newspapers have given the American public and the world the impression that I have only two alternatives in taking this stand: either I go to jail or go into the Army. There is another alternative and that alternative is justice. If justice prevails, if my Constitutional rights are upheld, I will be forced to go neither to the Army nor jail. . . .

— ALI'S PREPARED STATEMENT AFTER REFUSING
TO BE INDUCTED, APRIL 28, 1967

Nona Gaye on Belinda Ali

Ali's second wife, Belinda Boyd, was raised in the Muslim faith and married the Champ when she was just seventeen. According to Ali mythology, they met in the Muslim bakery where she worked, but that was just where the press first saw them together; they had actually met when she was just eleven. The combination of her youth and upbringing, and his noisy personality, made it easy for her to be the quiet, apparently subservient wife he wanted, and she was content to "do talking in the house," as she said. (Liberal fans of Ali find his unliberated view of women exasperating—just one of countless contradictory aspects of his personality.) But Belinda was a tall, strong woman with great inner strength as well; she was a good match for Ali for the time their marriage endured.

Nona Gaye, the rising actress and daughter of soul singer Marvin Gaye, plays Belinda in the Mann film, and like some of the other actors, she had met Ali earlier in her life. "He's more than a sports hero," says Gaye. "He transcended that just in the way he affects everybody. You hear him talk and you're captivated. I first met him as a little girl with my father, and when I saw him again after I'd gotten this part, he leaned over and whispered in my ear, 'You look just like your daddy.' I got all girly and silly. He's just got that charisma. He always had a fire and a passion for what he did.

You could tell how much he wanted to win, how confident he was that he was going to win. He just understood something. He just knew.

"My take on Belinda is that she was never intimidated by him. She was never really affected by how large he was and the way people stood back in awe of him. I think she just loved him like a wife loves her husband and wasn't afraid of how powerful his persona is to most people. And that played a part in her always telling him the truth and not sugar-coating anything. So I think he saw this woman who wasn't afraid of him, and that's what he loved about her. Her spunk, her fire. When you look at pictures of Belinda, that's all that you see— she's just a pillar of strength and poise."

Both an actress and a singer, following in the musical footsteps of her father, Gaye makes her feature film debut in *Ali*. She has been singing professionally since age 15 and recorded her first album at 18. She later had a successful career as a Ford Agency model while continuing her music recordings and performances.

ABOVE: Ali and Belinda, 1968. Photo Howard L. Bingham.

Ali's wife, Belinda, sat at the front of the bus. In Muslim dress with a skirt that came to her ankles, and a white cloth turban close to her head, she was a statuesque woman—precisely the word. Over six feet tall, as well proportioned as her husband, she had features sufficiently classic for the head of a Greek statue. In fact if these features were not one chiseled touch smaller than Ali's she could have been his sister in appearance or, better, his female surrogate. They would not have to live together for forty years to look alike. She was also a black belt in karate. She was also shy with strangers. She had the stiffness Black Muslims exhibit in the company of whites.

— NORMAN MAILER

He said he gave up being the prettiest on June 18, 1968, when Maryum was born. She was the first of the four children he had with Belinda, who by now had taken the Muslim name Khalilah.

— ROBERT LIPSYTE

He was my first love. He taught me everything I knew, and in the beginning he was beautiful. On the outside, he was always sure of himself, but inside I could tell there was a little insecurity. Not about his boxing; he was very secure at that. But in other ways, I think he was unsure of himself, and spent a lot of his life searching for who he was. . . .

God blessed us with four beautiful children. Maryum came first, about ten months after we were married. Then the twins—Rasheeda and Jamillah—were born, and finally, Muhammad Junior. Muhammad absolutely loved the children, but he didn't have the patience to spend full-time with them. He was good for about twenty minutes. "Oh, this baby is so sweet; she's so cute!" And then it was, "Please, take 'em." . . . But overall he was a good father, and we were very happy at first.

— BELINDA ALI

ABOVE: Ali and Belinda arrive in Zaire, 1974. Photo Howard L. Bingham.

Bundini:
Poet of the Streets

Drew (known as "Bundini") Brown met Ali in 1963. A poor kid from Florida, he had joined the Navy and then traveled the world with the merchant marine. He spent several years in the camp of the great middleweight champ Sugar Ray Robinson, and presented himself to Ali and Dundee as a peerless motivator, someone who could bring a generous helping of magic to Ali's quest for the championship. Bundini and Ali bonded deeply.

But with Bundini there were always problems. He went on drinking binges and enjoyed

the company of white women far too much for the Muslims around Ali. No one seems to know how many times he was married. Chronically broke and a natural hustler, he finally committed the unforgivable sin of pawning Ali's championship belt, getting himself kicked out of the entourage in mid-1965. The banishment lasted almost five years, but during his comeback, training to fight Jerry Quarry, Ali relented and brought him back. Bundini died of a stroke in 1988, the first member of the inner circle to pass on.

"To me, Ali was simply the best pure athlete there ever was," says Jamie Foxx, who plays Bundini in the film. "There's no sport out there that's as rough as boxing. Just him being the athlete he was made me think he was incredible. He was just pure energy—and style."

About Bundini's relationship with Ali, Foxx says, "They understood each other. You know, with every athlete and every star, there's always the guy that hangs around them. A big fish and a little fish that swims next to him. It's like Ali used Bundini as fuel when he was fighting. And Bundini kept it straight with him. He said, "You're losing, Champ, you're down. And you really need to come out and do this." Bundini was key in knowing how to stroke Ali's ego when he needed it, and at the same time give him the real deal.

"A guy walked up to me on the set once and said, 'Let me ask you something. Muhammad Ali is a hero of mine, and why would he have somebody like Bundini around?" Most people only see the outside of Bundini. But the inside stuff is that he really knew everything about boxing. He was with Sugar Ray Robinson for seven years, so he wasn't a hack when it came to boxing. He knew when a fighter was tired or run down, or when he needed what he would call spiritual help."

Foxx made an impressive dramatic film debut in Oliver Stone's *Any Given Sunday*. He also wrote, produced, and performed two songs for the film's best-selling soundtrack. Foxx's adeptness at moving from drama to comedy was demonstrated in the action comedy *Bait* directed by Antoine Fuqua. He also starred in the long-running television hit *The Jamie Foxx Show* and made his mark on small screen audiences alongside Jim Carrey and Damon Wayons on the sketch series *In Living Color*. His other feature film credits include *Booty Call*, *The Truth About Cats and Dogs*, and *The Great White Hype*.

LEFT: Ali and Drew "Bundini" Brown prepare for the "Rumble in the Jungle," Zaire, 1974. Photo Howard L. Bingham.

"Float like a butterfly,
sting like a bee..."

Bundini was a poet of the streets; a source of energy that Ali fed off constantly: someone who could put words together in a way that connoted exactly what he meant and Ali could understand. "Float like a butterfly; sting like a bee." That was Bundini. He used to say that Ali and the entourage were like a cake, made with flour, eggs, sugar, and that he, Bundini, was the nutmeg which gave it that little extra taste. If you caught Bundini in one of his drinking swings, which happened from time to time, there might be a problem. But sober, he was the sweetest, nicest guy in the world.

— DR. FERDIE PACHECO

Ali and Bundini Brown, Miami, 1965.
Photo Howard L. Bingham.

Ali on the Set

Since he is curious and gregarious by nature, it was no surprise that Muhammad Ali arranged to visit the film set several times. In Los Angeles, he dropped in on Will Smith's training gym in May 2000, before shooting even began, and was impressed by the slightly built actor's physical transformation into a heavyweight. In Chicago, he hung out and watched the filming at the Sinclair gas station set in his old neighborhood.

One of the Miami locations was the house where Ali used to live in the Overtown district. Shortly after the company finished filming there, Ali arrived in town and Howard Bingham took him back to visit the area where the Champ still has many friends. "He got a haircut at his old barbershop, ran into a few people he used to know and then wanted to see his old house," Bingham relates. "So he knocked on the door and apparently woke the owner up. The guy came to the door, holding his pants up with one hand and rubbing his eyes with the other. When he recognized who was on his doorstep, he nearly dropped his pants." As always, Ali drew crowds everywhere he went.

BELOW and ABOVE RIGHT: Ali with Will Smith and Michael Mann. RIGHT and INSET: Howard Bingham's 1964 photo of Ali with neighborhood kids at his Miami home, and one of the same girls (top left, standing) on his visit to the set in 2000. Photos Howard L. Bingham.

"Ali, boma ye!"

1974...

Ali's defeat by Joe Frazier—the first loss in his professional career—shocks the sports world and the wider world, which divides into those who rejoice and those who mourn. Ali, despite his philosophical words in the aftermath, is profoundly shaken yet just as deeply determined to continue his quest to recapture the title. His third opponent down this road is Ken Norton, whom Ali makes the error of taking too lightly. In round two, Norton's hard right breaks Ali's jaw—yet they keep fighting for the whole 12 rounds. Another setback. Meanwhile, as Ali trains for Frazier, the unthinkable happens: Smokin' Joe falls decisively in a title bout to a near-unknown, hard-punching young George Foreman.

So it's Ali vs. Frazier again—a slugfest in which neither does much damage or gains a clear advantage. But it's scored a narrow victory for Ali. Now at last, he's in a position to challenge Foreman for the championship. Up-and-coming promoter Don King has put together a deal that strikes everyone as crazy . . . except that it's for real. President Mobutu of Zaire has pledged $10 million to host the fight in his capital of Kinshasa. As King announces to the press his "Rumble in the Jungle," the clock starts on the most dramatic chapter of Ali's eventful life.

When Ali's plane lands in Kinshasa, his stature in the African homeland is instantly clear. Thousands of Zaireans line the airport roof, the fences, as close as they can get with security holding them back. They are chanting "Ali, boma ye!" (Ali, kill him!)—a refrain that will follow the former champ throughout the leadup to the fight. Foreman arrives, a hulking, hostile presence—and the international press, watching him wreak havoc on sparring partners and the heavy bag, predicts certain doom for Ali. Who, in public at least, shows only serene confidence. He's loving being in Africa, followed everywhere he goes by shouting kids, his victorious image painted on the walls of shanty housing behind Mobutu's sleek facade. And, in Belinda's absence, he finds a new female companion, the exotic Veronica Porche. It's the beginning of the end for his marriage, but that side of his life is pushed to the background for now.

Finally the night of October 25, 1974, arrives. It's a massive, joyous festival, with African dancers and American black music stars flown in to perform. Bundini whispers to Ali: "Forget every battle of man against man, of mind against mind, of soul against soul. This is the one. This is the greatest." The fighters enter the ring. The crowd takes up its chant. The battle begins. And Ali, alone with his destiny, defies all logic, all wisdom, following his unerring eyes and instinct and heart to an end no one could have dreamed: a knockout of Foreman in round eight.

The skies break; the rain comes. Zaire celebrates with ecstatic abandon. And Ali, out by himself for a walk, spars playfully with a kid in the African dawn.

Sports Illustrated

MARCH 18, 1971 · 50 CENTS

END OF THE ALI LEGEND

The whole time I wasn't allowed to fight, no matter what the authorities said, it felt like I was the heavyweight champion of the world. Then I lost to Joe Frazier. And what hurt most wasn't the money that losing cost me. It wasn't the punches I took. It was knowing that my title was gone. When I beat Sonny Liston, I was too young to appreciate what I'd won. But when I lost to Frazier, I would have done anything except go against the will of Allah to get my title back again.

— MUHAMMAD ALI

Each time Frazier and Ali fought, they gave us great memories. These two guys made the heavyweight division what it is today. I don't think there will ever be another decade of great heavyweights like it was back in the sixties and seventies.

— JAMES TONEY, FORMER MIDDLEWEIGHT CHAMPION,
WHO PLAYS JOE FRAZIER IN THE FILM

Coming Back

Ali kept fighting after he lost to Frazier—in fact he fought fourteen times in the next three years, an unusually active schedule. He fought every heavyweight contender available, from his old sparring partner and boyhood friend, Jimmy Ellis, to his old enemy, Floyd Patterson. He fought and whipped Jerry Quarry again. He beat the tall, lean, light-heavyweight champion, Bob Foster, but suffered his very first cut, a slash over his left eye that required five stitches to close.... He never fought for less than $200,000 a bout, and sometimes for twice as much, or more. His total ring earnings for those fourteen fights were more than $5 million, an incredible sum for a man who wasn't even the champion.

— ROBERT LIPSYTE

What happened against Norton might have happened at any stage of Ali's career, but promoters don't always know things like that. Ali's old nemesis, Eddie Futch, the demon trainer, was in Norton's corner and he had a new trick up his sleeve, like the Joker in Batman comics. He figured that Ali was so proud of his fast jab that if you jab back more or less simultaneously, he will be nonplussed.

And so it came to pass. Simple as it seems, this tactic is very unorthodox and Ali could not adjust to it. Norton held up his right glove to protect against Ali's left and shot his own back into the empty space. And Ali thought Norton's jab was actually faster than his. It wasn't, says Futch, but it didn't have to be. Ali's vanity was stung and his poise shaken.

— WILFRID SHEED

Losing to Norton was the end of the road, at least as far as I could see. Certainly, it was the worst moment I shared with Ali until those awful beatings at the end of his career. So many of Ali's fights had incredible symbolism, and here it was again. Ken Norton, a former Marine, in the ring against the draft dodger in San Diego, a conservative naval town. Richard Nixon had just been reelected with a huge mandate. . . . After that loss, it seemed as though Ali would never get his title back again.

— HOWARD COSELL

PAGE 98: Muhammad Ali in Zaire with President Mobutu Sese Seko, 1974. Photo Howard L. Bingham. PAGE 99: Will Smith as Ali with Michael Michele, who plays Veronica Porche. OPPOSITE: James Toney as Joe Frazier defeats Ali in the film's depiction of what some called "The Fight of the Century," and Sports Illustrated*'s cover of the actual fight. THIS PAGE, LEFT: Ali defeats Jerry Quarry, Atlanta, 1970, photo Howard L. Bingham, and (above) the same fight in the film, with Robert Sale as Jerry Quarry.*

Don King's
"Rumble in the Jungle"

To many, Don King seemed like an unlikely person to be masterminding a fight between the heavyweight titleholder and the most famous former champ ever. He had been in the numbers racket in Cleveland and served four years in prison for manslaughter. It was from there that he heard the broadcast of the first Ali-Frazier fight. He had no background in the boxing world. Amazingly, just four years later he had become one of the nation's most successful black businessmen—thanks to his connection with Ali, whom he had met through fellow Clevelander and recording artist Lloyd Price.

King's sleazy past and personal ambition often obscured a real drive to help the African-American community; his bond with Ali began when he convinced the Champ to appear in a boxing exhibition to benefit a black hospital in Cleveland. Boxing needed a black promoter, and King, with his business savvy, came along at the right time. After promoting some smaller fights, he got involved with the Foreman–Norton championship bout, but his dream was to match Ali and Foreman. The challenge: Ali's camp, once again led by Herbert Muhammad, wanted an unheard-of $5 million. King wasn't fazed but he warned that the fight would have to take place overseas to earn that much.

The real power behind the deal with Zaire was a company called Video Techniques (the closed-circuit broadcaster)—King was the front man. The total prize of $10 million, split between the two fighters, was the most ever for a fight; Mobutu Sese Seko was ready to part with his country's capital to gain visibility for Zaire and glory for himself. Ali flew to Zaire in early September 1974 with a 35-member entourage and settled in. The fight was scheduled for September 25, 3 A.M., to accommodate viewing times in the U.S.

"Don is larger than life by two hundred percent," claims actor Mykelti Williamson, who plays King. "I think he's a modern-day antihero. I was introduced to him by Howard Bingham and spent a couple of days in Las Vegas, hanging out with Don and watching him behave. And misbehave. He is a very powerful man, and you sense that when he walks into a room. In spite of his famous hairstyle, he's not a cartoon by any stretch of the imagination. He's to be taken very seriously.

"Don King was the first promoter to give professional fighters a shot at becoming millionaires. And although certain things about him may be questionable, he does fulfill the American dream. That's why he always uses the phrase, 'Only in America.'

"In the script, Belinda Ali says that King talks black, lives white and thinks green. Well, Don King is the ultimate capitalist. It's about the money. I mean, he's no different than Bill Gates. He just came from much more humble beginnings."

Mykelti Williamson costarred in *Three Kings* and is best known for his role as Benjamin "Bubba" Bufford-Blue in the Academy Award–winning *Forrest Gump.* He was also featured in Michael Mann's *Heat*, and one of his earliest acting breaks was on Mann's series *Miami Vice*. Williamson's other major film credits include *Gideon, Primary Colors, Con Air, How to Make an American Quilt, Free Willy, Free Willy 2: The Adventure Home*, and *Waiting to Exhale*. On television, Williamson starred in the series *The Fugitive* and *The Hoop Life* as well as the movie-of-the-week *The Delany Sisters' First 100 Years* and the Showtime cable production of *12 Angry Men*.

ABOVE: Mykelti Williamson as Don King. OPPOSITE: Don King in Zaire, 1974. Photo Howard L. Bingham.

King had magical eyes. Until one met him, it was hard to understand how he could possibly have managed to bring the fighters together, for he had few financial resources to match an event of this scope. King, however, had the ability to take all his true love (which given his substantial Black presence was not necessarily small) plus all of his false love, and pour them out through his eyes, his lambent eyes. . . . [H]e had approached Ali and Foreman with the splendid credentials of a fight manager whose two best fighters, Earnie Shavers and Jeff Merritt, had just both been knocked out in the first round. Still, he offered to promote Ali–Foreman. Each fighter would get five million dollars, he said. Those eyes of true love must have made the sum believable, for they glowed doubtless with the cool delights of lemonade, the fantasies of Pernod, and the golden kernels of corn—somehow, those eyes took him through barriers—he convinced Herbert Muhammad that he could produce this fight. "I reminded him of the teaching of his father Elijah Muhammad that every qualified Black man should be given a chance by his fellow Black men."

— NORMAN MAILER

For five million dollars, Ali will fight anywhere on the planet Earth.

— HERBERT MUHAMMAD TO DON KING

All you boys who don't take me seriously, who think George Foreman is going to whup me; when you get to Africa, Mobutu's people are gonna put you in a pot, cook you, and eat you.

— A CLASSIC SHOOT-FROM-THE-HIP ALI REMARK TO THE PRESS WHEN THE FIGHT WAS FIRST ANNOUNCED. ZAIRE'S FOREIGN MINISTER DEPLORED IT AS HARMFUL TO HIS COUNTRY'S IMAGE.

Thursday, five days before the bout, Ali gave a typical seminar. "This fight is going to be not only the largest boxing eee-vent, but it will prove to be the largest eee-vent in the history of the world. It will be the greatest upset of which anyone has ever heard, and to those who are ignorant of boxing, it will seem like the greatest miracle. The boxing public are fools and illiterates to the knowledge and art of boxing. This is because you here who write about boxing are ignorant of what you try to describe. You writers are the real fools and illiterates. I am going to demonstrate—so you will have something new for your columns—why I cannot be defeated by George Foreman and will create the greatest upset in the history of boxing which you by your ignorance and foolishness as writers have actually created."

— NORMAN MAILER

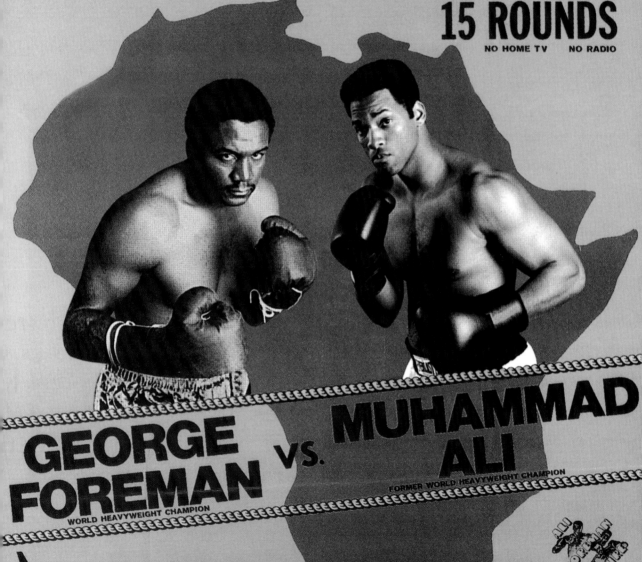

The Homecoming

Mr. President, I've been a citizen of the United States of America for 33 years and was never invited to the White House. It sure gives me pleasure to be invited to the Black House.

— ALI ON MEETING PRESIDENT MOBUTU AT THE PRESIDENTIAL PALACE IN KINSHASA

In Zaire, everything was black—from the train drivers and the hotel owners to the teachers in the schools and the pictures on the money. It was just like any other society, except it was black, and because I'm black oriented and a Muslim, I was home there. . . . I could name you a thousand things I saw that made me feel good.

— ALI ON HIS TIME IN ZAIRE, *PLAYBOY* INTERVIEW, NOVEMBER, 1975

OPPOSITE: One of several murals created by the Ali art department and a local artist to represent children's drawings on the walls of Zairean shantytowns, rooting Ali on before the fight. BELOW: Ali arrives in Zaire, 1974. Photo Howard L. Bingham.

Watching Ali in Zaire was wonderful. He'd go on walks into areas where I don't think they had electricity, let alone television sets, and everyone knew him. To see the looks on people's faces when they saw him, the love, the power he had over them; it was spine-tingling.

— DR. FERDIE PACHECO

Foreman the Invincible

When 25-year-old George Foreman took the crown from Joe Frazier, he knocked Frazier down six times in just two rounds. No one could remember ever seeing a fighter punch harder. He had demolished most of his opponents in the first three rounds, and had started referring to round three as his "murder round." So even though Ali hungered for a title fight against Foreman, virtually no one gave him a chance to win. Foreman "had never even been knocked off his feet in a prizefight," writes Robert Lipsyte. "Ali, now thirty-two, considered to be in the twilight of his career, could no longer even depend on his greatest gift—his once-dazzling speed."

Seeing George Foreman today, a jolly giant chatting up talk show hosts or pitching his cooking equipment on TV, it's nearly impossible to recognize the silent, often surly, media-wary young man who came to Africa to fight Ali in 1974. "Other champions had a presence larger than themselves," Norman Mailer comments. "They offered charisma. Foreman had silence. It vibrated about him in silence."

Foreman is played in the film by current world-ranked heavyweight Charles Shufford, who says he and Will Smith watched a tape of the climactic fight "maybe 100 times." Shufford, ironically, had to adapt his own style, which he modeled partly on Ali, to that of Foreman. "I watch a lot of Ali tapes, try to throw a lot of his game in my game. And other older fighters: Sugar Ray Robinson, Joe Louis—kind of mix it all together with my own stuff. Ali was the first boxer I really started watching and emulating his style.

"Foreman, though, was mostly about a lot of power and wide shots. It's more like looping shots; he kind of fought with his hands out here, blocking. My style is totally different than Foreman's. But a lot of his stuff I might throw into my game. That wouldn't be a bad idea."

It is punishing for a boxer to have a long workout on a heavy bag. It hurts one's arms, it hurts one's head, it can spring one's knuckles if the hands are not wrapped. Big as a tackling dummy, the bag weighs eighty pounds or more, and when a punch is not thrown properly, the boxer's body shudders with the shock. It is like being brought down by an unexpected tackle. One bad punch. Now Foreman began to hit this bag with lefts and rights. He did not throw them slowly, he did not throw them fast, he threw them steadily, putting all of his body into each punch, which came to mean that he was contracting and expelling his force forty to fifty times a minute for he threw that many punches, not fast, not slow, but concussive in their power. . . . Each of these blows was enough to smash an average athlete's ribs; anybody with poor stomach muscles would have a broken spine. Foreman hit the heavy bag with the confidence of a man who can pick up a sledgehammer and knock down a tree. The bag developed a hollow as deep as his head. . . . [B]oom!. . . . boom!. . . . boom!. . . . went the sounds of his fists into the bag, methodical, rhythmic, and just as predictably hypnotic as the great overhead blow of the steam hammer driving a channel of steel into clay.

— NORMAN MAILER

ABOVE: Charles Shufford as George Foreman.
OPPOSITE: Foreman at the weigh-in in Kinshasa, 1974.
Photo Howard L. Bingham.

"I never get a chance to talk much in the ring. By the time I begin to know a fellow, it's over."
— GEORGE FOREMAN BEFORE THE FIGHT

On Location: Africa

From Miami, where the *Ali* production finished shooting in the U.S., it was a 17-hour journey by air to Johannesburg, South Africa. From Johannesburg to Maputo, Mozambique, where the Zaire scenes were filmed, was a one-hour flight—from the first world to the third.

"This was my first time on the continent of Africa," Will Smith recalls. "And when we got off the plane, there was this black dude driving the bus and he said, 'Welcome home, brothers.' And I was like, 'Oh, go ahead with the welcome home, man; come on with the welcome home.' It was just one of those moments of truth and purity and love."

Although the Rumble in the Jungle took place in Kinshasa, Zaire, that country is now Congo, currently one of the most politically unstable nations on the continent. It was evident that the movie couldn't be filmed there.

"Michael fell in love with the architecture in Maputo," explains associate producer Guzmano Cesaretti, a fine arts photographer who has worked with Mann since the film *Jericho Mile*. "It was mostly built by the Portuguese during the middle to later 1900s. There are buildings with wonderful Art Deco–style curves and arches

alongside some with straight lines from the block-style buildings of the 1960s. All very aged and weatherbeaten. It looked very much the way Kinshasa was in the 1970s photos we saw."

There had never been a major movie filmed here. There were a great many concerns about being the first. "Much of the infrastructure of Mozambique had been destroyed by the Portuguese when they left [in 1975] and, right after that, the country suffered 15 years of civil war that did even more damage," Cesaretti explains. "Then, earlier this year, Mozambique was devastated by floods that wiped out roads and bridges, dislodged land mines, and washed away houses. But the worst was in the north—mostly pretty far from where we were planning to film."

However, there was flooding in Marracuene, an area about 60 miles north of Maputo, where plans had been made to re-create the N'Sele

ABOVE: Location montage of Independence Square in Accra, the capital of Ghana—an important symbol of African black nationalism. OPPOSITE: Don King (Mykelti Williamson) greets the crowds at Kinshasa Airport (filmed in Maputo, Mozambique).

compound—a place on the outskirts of Kinshasha where Ali had stayed back in 1964. Consequently, the production had to divide the filming among three locations. The interiors were shot in Key Biscayne, Florida, and a high school gymnasium in Maputo that architecturally matched the N'Sele gym. For the exterior, the production built a replica of the compound in Marracuene as soon as the flooding subsided.

Health concerns also arose from the floodwaters. A few members of the construction crew

ABOVE: The N'Sele compound at Marracuene, outside Maputo.

came down with malaria and had to be hospitalized. But by the time filming had begun, the shooting crew had been forewarned and forearmed with medication and repellent, and cooler weather killed off many of the mosquitoes.

One of the major exterior locations in Maputo was an area called Mavalane A, just outside the airport. Flying into Maputo, one can see this vast labyrinth of huts and unpaved roads, but only from the ground can one gauge the depth of the community's poverty. Some in Mavalane A have electricity and concrete walls; most live under roofs of scrap tin and plastic supported by sticks bound with wire.

Most of those living in Mavalane had never seen a movie, let alone seen one being filmed. But hundreds of residents lined the narrow dirt streets to watch "Ali" as he jogged through town on his pre-fight workouts. Some had heard of Will Smith—mainly through his music—but few knew he was a movie star. As filming continued here over three days, Smith's interaction with the crowds won him new fans. But the extent of the bond he was forging didn't become fully clear until after the last shot on the final day there.

"There were about 60 kids [hired extras] running down the street alongside me, shouting 'Ali boma ye!' and we'd been doing variations on that over the past few days, felt like 60 times," recalls Smith. "We got to the end of the last day and Michael called 'Wrap,' and we were saying goodbye, and they just started getting excited, you know, the way kids do. I started dancing, they started dancing; we're playing, I'm singing and they start chanting and, all of a sudden, the kids just picked me up and started carrying me through the streets.

"It was weird; I didn't feel like they were carrying me because I was famous. It just felt like we had connected in some emotional way, in some way that was really spiritual. It gave me a great sense of what Ali must have felt the first time he came to Africa. And it really inspired me to want to live up to that kind of adulation."

But if the reward came first, the punishment was to come later: eight days shooting eight rounds of one of the most punishing fights of Ali's career.

Northwest of Maputo is Machava Stadium. Built during the Portuguese colonial period, it has hosted international soccer tournaments that filled

its 64,000-seat capacity. However, the stadium had not seen a capacity crowd for any event in some time and, like many public facilities in this impoverished nation, had fallen into disrepair. Before filming could begin, the production had to make over $100,000 worth of improvements to the building. They also had to repair and upgrade roads leading to the stadium. The stadium had no electrical power, so the company had to import 12 generators from South Africa.

The art department constructed 30,000 cardboard cutouts to fill out the crowd, but another 10,000 live bodies were needed for the big scene when Ali makes his entrance. It was decided to send out fliers inviting people throughout Maputo to "watch the filming." On the night of Ali's big entrance, more than 30,000 people showed up.

BELOW: Location-scout montage of Machava Stadium in Maputo. RIGHT: Set construction at the stadium, with cardboard cut-outs of spectators in the stands.

The Once and Future Champ

Early in the morning of October 30, after 55 days of waiting, Ali finally stepped into the ring to meet George Foreman, with 60,000 Africans in the stadium cheering him on. What happened in the next hour has become legend. Ali surprised everyone by coming out of his corner punching hard and, 30 seconds into round two, by getting on the ropes and staying there most of the remainder of the fight. He let Foreman wear himself down while he miraculously avoided countless blows and absorbed many others—then attacked furiously in round eight and knocked Foreman down and out with perhaps the best punch of his lifetime.

Michael Mann, Will Smith, and everyone else involved with the production were determined that their re-creation of this stirring event would be as thrilling and true to the spirit of the original as film can achieve.

"For Will's entrance, I specifically ordered him kept out of the arena until it was time to do the shot and roll film," says Mann. "When he finally did enter, it was to the spontaneous eruption of 30,000 people, reacting en masse to his charisma and to that of Ali. I think that energy comes through in the film. You can see the impact on Will's face and feel the authenticity of that moment in his performance."

Spontaneity was almost carried to dangerous extremes in the stands, however. The huge crowd overran food and water tables set up to provision about half their number (the turnout that had been hoped for). Somehow, the security force of more than 100 Mozambican police, along with an army of cool-headed production assistants, managed to maintain the peace and prevent the kind of soccer riot that had killed 50 people only weeks earlier in South Africa.

The security forces weren't the only embattled figures in Machava Stadium. Night after night for eight nights, from sundown to sunup, two boxers were reenacting one of the most famed fights in ring history.

"Each round in a fight is a drama, and for rounds one and two the drama was, will Ali survive the third?" says Mann. "He almost didn't. Foreman put everything he had into that round, and every time Ali was able to avert his head enough to turn a deadly shot into a glancing blow, it was like a counterpunch to Foreman's psyche."

Ali's strategy was to let Foreman wear himself out swinging at him. In playing that through, he took a pounding not only in that round but in the ones that preceded and followed. "Foreman was the most devastating puncher in boxing," notes Smith. "And Ali's plan was, 'O.K., I'm gonna let him hit me as hard as he can until he gets tired.'

That's a dumb plan; it's a terrible plan. It's just plain bad. Except it worked."

And it hurt—both in the historical fight and in its cinematic recreation. Once the adrenaline started pumping in the ring, emotions drew little distinction between real life and the movies.

"I was hitting him pretty good," says Charles Shufford, who plays Foreman, of Smith. "I mean, Michael wanted it to look real, he wanted this to be the best boxing movie ever. And Will told me, 'Go ahead and throw them; don't fake the punches in there.' He's in good shape and he knows how to box. We'd go ahead and throw them, both of

us. We didn't throw them the same to the head like you would in a match, but we'd throw them pretty good to the body."

"I figure it's only about one out of every ten body shots that gets in, and a lot of fans wonder why boxers waste a lot of time and energy in punching the body," Smith reports. "But when you get hit with a clean body shot, you wish to God sometimes he would have punched you in your nose. You get hit with a clean body shot, it shuts everything down. Worst part is, you can't let on to your opponent that he hurt you. I had about six or seven of those in performing this fight. Now that's acting!"

But Smith survived and Ali prevailed, just as he had 27 years earlier. As the production wound down, the filming hours grew longer as Michael Mann pushed to make his schedule. Then midway through the sixth brutal week of cold, buggy nights and hot, dusty days in Mozambique, nearly five months after filming had begun, it was suddenly over. A handful of crew and cast flew to Accra, Ghana, for one day of shooting there. Everyone else flew home.

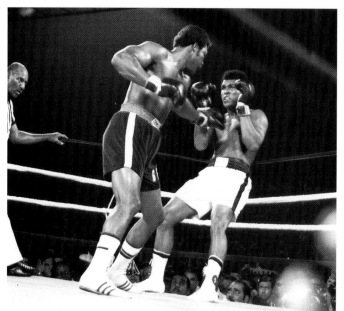

LEFT: Ali practicing his famous "rope-a-dope" strategy against Foreman in their 1974 fight. Photo Howard L. Bingham.
ABOVE: The same maneuver enacted by Will Smith as Ali and Charles Shufford as Foreman.

The bell! Through a long unheard sigh of collective release, Ali charged across the ring. He looked as big and determined as Foreman, so he held himself, as if *he* possessed the true threat. They collided without meeting, their bodies still five feet apart. Each veered backward like similar magnetic poles repelling one another forcibly. Then Ali came forward again, Foreman came forward, they circled, they feinted, they moved in an electric ring, and Ali threw the first punch, a tentative left. It came up short. Then he drove a lightning-strong right straight as a pole into the stunned center of Foreman's head, the unmistakable thwomp of a high-powered punch. A cry went up. Whatever else happened, Foreman had been hit. No opponent had cracked George this hard in years and no sparring partner had dared to.

· · ·

Up and down the press rows, one exclamation was leaping, "He's hitting him with *rights*." Ali had not punched with such authority in seven years. Champions do not hit other champions with right-hand leads. Not in the first round.

· · ·

With twenty seconds left to the [eighth] round, Ali attacked. By his own measure, by that measure of twenty years of boxing, with the knowledge of all he had learned of what could and could not be done at any instant in the ring, he chose this as the occasion and lying on the ropes, he hit Foreman with a right and left, then came off the ropes to hit him with a left and a right. Into this last right hand he put his glove and his forearm again, a head-stupefying punch that sent Foreman reeling forward. As he went by, Ali hit him on the side of the jaw with a right, and darted away from the ropes in such a way as to put Foreman next to them. For the first time in the entire fight he had cut off the ring on Foreman. Now Ali struck him a combination of punches fast as the punches of the first round, but harder and more consecutive, three capital rights in a row struck Foreman, then a left, and for an instant on Foreman's face appeared the knowledge that he was in danger and must start to look to his last protection. His opponent was attacking, and there were no ropes behind the opponent. What a dislocation: the axes of his existence were reversed! He was the man on the ropes! Then a big projectile exactly the size of a fist in a glove drove into the middle of Foreman's mind, the best punch of the startled night, the blow Ali saved for a career . . . . He went over like a six-foot sixty-year-old butler who has just heard tragic news, yes, fell over all of a long collapsing two seconds, down came the Champion in sections and Ali revolved with him in a close circle, hand primed to hit him one more time, and never the need, a wholly intimate escort to the floor.

— Norman Mailer

FADE IN:

EXT. MIAMI STREET – MOVEMENT – NIGHT (1964)

in the dark. Coming toward us. Up and down in sync to an INSTRUMENTAL LEAD-IN from somewhere. A slip of light. A glimpse of somebody in shadow under a sweatshirt hood, staring at us, in and out of the dark as...

INT. THE STAGE, HAMPTON HOUSE CLUB – EMPTY FRAME – NIGHT

A man walks into the shot, grabs a microphone, slips out of his jacket and looks at us. He wants to tell us something. He's in a lavender light. This is SAM COOKE. What he calls out...a throaty mixture of gospel, soul and sex...is "Let me hear it!" And WOMEN SHRIEK. He says, "Yeah!" They answer, shrieking, "Oh, yeah!"...

EXT. MIAMI STREET – HOODED MAN'S FACE – NIGHT

up and down, running along a dark road in the dead of night, passing vacant lots with debris amid trees and faded buildings. He is CASSIUS CLAY. He runs in construction boots. His eyes stare from under the hood. He passes the husk of an abandoned car, a pastel storefront. We're in Overtown, Miami's inner-city black neighborhood.

INT. THE STAGE, HAMPTON HOUSE CLUB (MIAMI) – SAM COOKE

shouts, "Don't fight it! We gonna feel it!" The women in the audience answer: "Gotta feel it!"

EXT. MIAMI STREET – CASSIUS – NIGHT

now runs diagonally across NW 7th INTERCUT with Cooke shouting, "Yeah!"

EXT. MACARTHUR CAUSEWAY – CASSIUS – NIGHT

> **SAM COOKE'S AUDIENCE** (O.S.)
> Oh, yeah!

Cassius runs toward us. Off to the side is the black-mirrored water of Biscayne Bay, leaden clouds in a black sky. And now Sam Cooke SINGS "...because you make me wanna mooove...!" and breaks into the first verse of "Feel It." But we see Cassius' eyes are FO-

---

NOTE: This printed screenplay is as accurate as possible but may not in all cases reflect the final cut of the film seen in theaters, as editing was still in progress when the book went to press.

CUSED, CONCENTRATED, ELSEWHERE. To where is this man running? Why is his expression so distant? A WHITE LIGHT suddenly hits him from behind. He looks over at...

WIDE FROM THE FRONT: CASSIUS + A METRO-DADE POLICE CAR

that's slowed, clocking the suspicious, running black man. The driver starts to pull over, to hassle Cassius. Then, the cop riding shotgun gets a radio call. He taps the driver's shoulder. They take off, the driver laughing. Cassius looks after the white cops. He is neither relieved nor angry. He's dismissive. And, instead, he sees something else...

INT. A BOARD ROOM – GORDON DAVIDSON – DAY

and six other patrician, white businesspeople of Louisville in their green baize and wood-paneled Luxo boardroom. They speak soundlessly and patronizingly to Cassius Clay, Sr., seated at the foot of the table. It relates to the stack of contracts in front of him. He is in a suit and tie, his hair and moustache are dapper. His tie's a little loud. He has his hands folded deferentially in front of him.

> **LSG BOARD MEMBER**
> (reading)
> "...the successor trustee shall be fully authorized to pay or disperse such sums from the income or principal as may be required."
> (beat)
> Do you understand so far, Mr. Clay?

> **CASSIUS CLAY, SR.**
> Uh, yes, I do.

We get the impression that, if he doesn't understand what he's being told, he's faking it. He is conforming, delivering socially mandated deference...

FRONTAL: CASSIUS, SR.

and BEYOND HIM, seated against the wall, is Cassius, Jr. in sport jacket and tie. Right now he looks to his left and to the right, and only then do we notice the entire wall he's against is covered with pictures of thoroughbreds and studs this Louisville Sponsoring Group owns as well. He is one among their sporting possessions. He doesn't like it. He looks at the back of his father listening.

> **LSG BOARD MEMBER**
> Are you sure, sir?

> **CASSIUS CLAY, SR.**
> Yeah. I follow you.

> **LSG BOARD MEMBER**
> Okay. 'Cause I'd be happy to explain any of these terms.

> **CASSIUS CLAY, SR.**
> No, thank you.

> **LSG BOARD MEMBER**
> Thank you, sir.

EXT. MACARTHUR CAUSEWAY – CLOSER: CASSIUS' EYES – NIGHT

back here, now, crossing through black night and over black water of the MacArthur Causeway. We start to HEAR pop pop pop pop pop pop pop POP over Sam Cooke's music, and Sam Cooke's image SUPERIMPOSES as he segues from "Feelin'" to "Bring It On Home." And the pop pop pop pop pop carries us into...

INT. THE FIFTH STREET GYM, (MIAMI) – SPEED BAG – DAWN

Cassius' fists fly in a reeling motion, hitting the speed bag. But it's his eyes that arrest us...focused, concentrated.

OVER CASSIUS' SHOULDER: BROWN SPEED BAG

is a blur. And it SLOWS and becomes a brown boxing glove driving in a SLOWED straight line right at us like a piston. OVER the glove, pushing the fist at us is SONNY LISTON. The brown glove hits...

INT. RING – A BOXER (N.D. BOXER)

in a linear left jab. These punches are watched by Cassius' eyes in the Fifth Street Gym...studiously studying Liston's feet...straight-line movement...the jab, linear and straight at us. But it SLAMS into the Boxer, not Cassius. Down he goes. He's out. The referee pulls out his mouthpiece. It's a bloody mess. Teeth have been knocked out with it, so devastating is Sonny Liston... A distant crowd ROARS.

INT. RING – CASSIUS – NIGHT

VERY CLOSE, climbs into the crush with other contenders. Victorious, Liston, being escorted out, passes very close to him on purpose to say...

> **SONNY LISTON**
> (whispers; low)
> Gonna fuck you up. Gonna beat you like I's your daddy...

To Cassius, boxing is dangerous athletics, but Liston's malevolence is straight from the street.

INT. FIFTH STREET GYM - CASSIUS' EYES
SEE...

INT. CHURCH - THE BACK OF HIS FATHER'S HEAD

working. He's painting a mural. It's the face of WHITE JESUS with blue eyes and blonde hair. CASSIUS, SR.'S EYES painting... EYES OF 12-YEAR-OLD CASSIUS, JR. watching white Jesus go up on the Negro Baptist Church in Louisville become...

INT. FIFTH STREET GYM - CASSIUS' EYES

watching now...

INT. A CITY BUS - WATCHING - DAY

the back of his own head moving through a tunnel of white faces, holding his mother's hand, passing the balloon faces of nice white passengers, teenagers in athletic sweaters going to high school, some children, all seated. MOVING through to the rear of the bus where, standing, are black women, heavyset with heavy legs, and middle-aged black men with large, rough hands, crowded on their way to the day's labor or domestic jobs in the back of the bus.

12-YEAR-OLD CASSIUS LOOKS

at a newspaper being refolded by one man in front of his face...

CASSIUS' POV: LOUISVILLE COURIER: EMMETT TILL

Published nationwide, it shows his gouged-out eye, the barbed wire noose around his neck, the mutilation to his face because at 14 years old he winked at a white girl in Alabama.

CASSIUS, JR.

is frozen by the image. It will haunt him for most of his life. The man holding the paper sees the boy's fear and pushes the paper out at him as a rough joke. Cassius reacts. Then, the man rises and offers his seat to Odessa. Then someone shouts...

> **ANGELO DUNDEE**
> TIME!

INT. FIFTH STREET GYM - CASSIUS

PAST him a short man in a white shirt, ANGELO DUNDEE, has entered with a folded newspaper under his arm.

And Cassius—elsewhere—SLAMS the speed bag with a right hook, and the bag becomes...

INT. THE MASJID AL ANSAR-MOSQUE - CASSIUS - DAY (MIAMI)

in black glasses, leaning against a wall.

> **MALCOLM X** (O.S.)
> ...and those of you who think you came here to hear us tell you, like these Negro leaders do, that times will get better and we shall overcome someday, I tell you: you came to the wrong place.

MALCOLM X is at the podium. Ceiling fans. We could be in Tripoli.

> **MALCOLM X** (Cont'd)
> 'Cause your times will never get better until you make them better. And any of you who think you came here to hear us tell you to turn the other cheek to the brutality of the white man and the established system of injustice in this country, to beg for your place at their lunch counter, I say again! You came to the wrong place.

And Cassius is there in a black shirt, standing in the back. Malcolm X sees him, nods...the casualness attests their familiarity is close and extensive...

> **MALCOLM X** (Cont'd)
> (beat)
> 'Cause we don't teach you to turn the other cheek. We don't teach you to turn the other cheek in the South. We don't teach you to turn the other cheek in the North. The Honorable Elijah Muhammad teaches you, instead, to obey the law. To carry yourselves in a respectable way. And a proud Afro-American way. But at the same time...we teach you...that anyone who puts his hand on you? Do your BEST... to see he doesn't PUT HIS HAND on any...body...else...AGAIN.

INT. FIFTH STREET GYM - LUMINOUS HOOP - MORNING

Whopwhopwhopwhopwhop...as first rays of golden light illuminate the jump rope spinning effortlessly over his head in a blur. Dust dances in light through the two dirty windows with boxing gloves and "Fifth Street Gym" painted on them. It's that time of day Jack Johnson called the "fighter's hour," "...between the night and the light..." ...whopwhopwhopwhopwhop... And Angelo Dundee puts on a pot of coffee. He washes his hands in a dirty sink, thoroughly drying them.

Alert and clean, he's old school. He goes back to the edge of the ring, reading his newspaper. Now, crossing past the white windows is DREW "BUNDINI" BROWN. He takes an orange out of his pocket, sitting on a bench, silently peels it... As Cassius "walks" the rope, jumping up and back.

> **ANGELO DUNDEE**
> (approving; past newspaper)
> Yeah. Like that, Daddy. Don't jump in one place. Bad for the heart. That's the most important thing.
> (without looking)
> TIME!

Cassius drops the rope where he stands, and walks off as Sam Cooke...

INT. THE HAMPTON HOUSE CLUB - SAM COOKE

segues into "Bring It On Home" and women in the front row reach out for him. The heat between Cooke and them is palpable. The first row is going crazy as...

INT. FIFTH STREET GYM - CASSIUS

sits into our frame, glistening with sweat, directed through tortuous calisthenics by the hands of Luis Sarria.

> **ANGELO DUNDEE**
> TIME!!!

INT. HAMPTON HOUSE CLUB - HIGH + WIDE FRONTAL: SAM COOKE'S

sweating. The place is rocking as...

INT. THE RING, FIFTH STREET GYM - CASSIUS' EYES - DAY

alive, sparring. But Cassius never throws a punch... He jerks back, sliding away, an inch away from being hit. He circles in a movement that seems off-balance and then becomes fluid and changes rate, faking out where you think he'll be. His sparring partner throws a jab that misses and follows with a hook. Cassius slips it by an inch. Entering the gym, now, is gregarious DR. FERDIE PACHECO with a young, afro'd HOWARD BINGHAM, who starts photographing while LUIS SARRIA looks at us. None of the gathered crowd, the greatest "corner" in boxing, breaks his concentration. He's in his zone. We're in the ring. Cassius, trance-like, hands down, circles and slips in no predictable way as...

INT. A LIMOUSINE - NOW CASSIUS IS - DAY

zenned-out in SLO-MO on the way somewhere in a suit and tie. People on the Miami streets drift by. The slow-moving limo floats on its soft suspension through the pastel heat of Miami. While Sam Cooke...

INT. HAMPTON HOUSE CLUB - SAM COOKE

drives to the big climax of "Bring It On Home To Me...!" counter to the limo's EXTREME CALM as Sam Cooke's medley ends and...

INT. A HALLWAY, THE MIAMI CONVENTION CENTER - CASSIUS - DAY

in a terry-cloth robe, walks faster and faster as Dundee and Bundini, Bingham and his cameras, Pacheco and RUDY race to keep up. And as Cassius slams through a door into a large room...

INT. THE WEIGH-IN ROOM, MIAMI CONVENTION CENTER - CASSIUS - DAY

EXPLODES:

CASSIUS/BUNDINI
(shout)
Float like a butterfly! Sting like a bee! Rumble, young man, rumble. Aaaaaaargh!

CASSIUS
Sonny Liston: you ain't no champ! You a chump!
(beat)
You want to lose your money, bet on Sonny. He know I'm great. He will go in eight!

500 press, promoters and boxing people turn and stare!

CASSIUS (Cont'd)
What you lookin' at, you ugly bear?!

LISTON a tree trunk in boxing shorts, can't wait to pull apart this kid.

CASSIUS (Cont'd)
C'mon, bum. I whup you right here!

Cassius pushes past people and leaps at Sonny! He wants to rumble right now. Bundini, Rudy, Dundee, Liston's handlers struggle to keep them apart, wrestle Cassius onto the scale.

A MAN
(reading)
... 210... Cassius Clay weighs 210 pounds.

CASSIUS
(changes down)
You sure you got that right...?

The man nods. Cassius gets off, is

pulled aside. And Liston gets on: unremitting stare of death at Cassius...

THE MAN
218. Sonny Liston...the heavyweight champion of the world weighs 218 pounds...

BUNDINI
Pounds of what?!

And Cassius goes off again...

CASSIUS
Pounds of ugly! He so ugly, sweat run backwards off his forehead to get away from his face! C'mon, bear! I turn you into a rug!! Rumble right now, man!

He's restrained by Angelo and Bundini.

SONNY LISTON
(low)
Keep talkin', punk-ass faggot! I'll fuck you up like I's your daddy...

Handlers break it up and hustle Liston out of there.

CASSIUS
You whup me, I'll crawl out of the ring on my knees and catch the next jet plane out of the country.

JIMMY CANNON
(older reporter)
That a promise?

Laughter.

CASSIUS
(to Jimmy Cannon)
...you be the first eatin' his words!

A Doctor claps a cuff around Cassius' arm, taking blood pressure.

THE DOCTOR
(alarmed, to Pacheco)
210 over 110?! I can't let him in the ring in this condition!

REPORTERS
(shout)
Liston says he'll talk with his fists. "Lip from Louisville."
(laughter)
...odds 7:1 against you. Big bet's whether he'll knock you out in the first round or third round or kill you altogether. You scared of him?

CASSIUS
I'm scared of no man. I give Sonny Liston talking lessons,

boxing lessons and falling down lessons.

CANNON/OTHERS
Yeah, sure. Are you a Black Mus-lim? Pat Putnam in the Miami Herald said...

CASSIUS
"Black Muslim"'s a press word...

Dundee's defensive, fast...

ANGELO DUNDEE
Man's religion's his own business. What kinda question's that?

REPORTERS/HOWARD COSELL
Does he hate white people? Malcolm X was in town. Then he left. Was that so he wouldn't embarrass you? Liston cannot stand you...

ANGELO DUNDEE
(sees)
Howard!

HOWARD COSELL
...cannot stand you, Cassius. He really wants to kill you...

HOWARD COSELL is balding, tall, forties, lugging a tape recorder.

CASSIUS
Howard Cosell, you are an instigator!
(Cosell smiles)
How you get that way? When I'm done with Sonny Liston, I'm comin' after you!

Dundee uses that to end the conference before it strays into "Black Muslim" territory. Meanwhile on the way out...

DOCTOR
(to Pacheco)
It doesn't come down, I cancel this fight. You call me in an hour with his blood pressure.

EXT./INT. MIAMI RENTAL HOUSE - DR. PACHECO - DAY

past guards, Bundini, press, starts to enter. Inside, Clay's on the sofa, in his underwear, watching "The Man With the X-Ray Eyes," who has the power to imbue and control from beams emitted from his eyes. Dundee and Bingham hang out.

Cassius' mind is elsewhere. His eyes float to the corner of the doorway before we see Pacheco, even though from the outside, has started to enter...

125

EXT. CASSIUS' RENTAL HOUSE, BACKYARD – CORNER OF HOUSE – DAY (MIAMI)

Nothing. Cassius is asleep in a lounge chair...incongruously a TV is run from the house by an extension cord. Cassius wakes. His eyes say, "Who are you?"

BUNDINI
(entering)
I'm called Bundini, rhymes with Houdini. He was a Jew, too... some other people call me Fastblack...or Daddy Mac...

Drew "Bundini" Brown, early forties, holds a hat in his hand, his eyes always seem to be glistening, ready to rage, laugh or cry, tentatively approaches. Cassius' flat eyes return to the television.

BUNDINI *(Cont'd)*
(motions at lounge chair)
Shorty sent me to Sugar Ray Robinson. I gave my power to Sugar Ray for seven years, gave him my voodoo, my magic. Now Shorty sent me to you.

CASSIUS
Who Shorty?

BUNDINI
I call him Shorty 'cause he like 'em circumcised. Original people. Like Moses. And I was a babe in a basket, too. I was born on a doorstep with a note 'cross my chest that read, "Do the best you can for him, world." I had to suck the first nipple come along. I didn't run away from home...I been runnin' to home.

Cassius should kick him out, but Bundini's got his foot in the door of Cassius' attention.

BUNDINI *(Cont'd)*
(beat, and his raison d'être)
Now, I gotta ask you. You fixin' them fights? Else no way you could tell great Archie Moore what round you droppin' him in...all of them predictions you make, comin' true. Never heard of nobody predictin' the round like you. You either a phony or Shorty's in your corner. Tell me the truth, young man...

Cassius, stretched out, mumbles without looking at him...

CASSIUS
...I study every fight. 'Til I got a plan. Wear him down two through four. Drop him in the fifth round. So the p'diction ain't a p'diction. It's a plan. And 'cause of all the poppin' off I do, I know I gotta win! That's the truth. And why I'm tellin' you?

BUNDINI
'Cause I'm gonna be your Inspiration. Your motivator. In your corner. Can I be in your corner, young man?

CASSIUS
(thinks, then)
Yeah...

BUNDINI
(inexplicably moved, covers)
Ain't spent much time in Miami. Where the water?

Cassius has drifted off, back to watching TV. What he sees as his eyes close is:

INT. MIAMI RENTAL HOUSE – PACHECO

The blur of Pacheco taking his blood pressure. Now Cassius looks and his shaman, Bundini, enters.

PACHECO
120 over 80?
(re: his blood pressure)
You should be asleep...

The weigh-in episode was an act. We take a different measure of this man. Pacheco sits next to Cassius and eats some of his potato chips.

INT. MIAMI CONVENTION CENTER, A DRESSING ROOM – HANDS – EARLY EVENING

being wrapped. Cassius' shirt is off, sitting on a bench in the dressing room...the ritualistic tradition, having his hands taped. Dundee expertly does it. In the background, Bundini, Pacheco, Bingham, Rudy and Two Men in dark suits, someone from Liston's camp, and a State Boxing Inspector watch. Then, the door opens for Malcolm X, in a dark suit, thin tie. Cassius lights up. Dundee is done. The Boxing Inspector signs the tape. Then, Dundee puts on gloves and laces them while...

CASSIUS
When you get back?

MALCOLM X
Just now. I'm front row, seat 7.

RUDY
I'm gonna find Mom and Dad.

CASSIUS
You could have stayed. Nobody gotta hide when they with me.

MALCOLM X
Nothing wrong with being cool, my brother. You been working toward this moment for four years.

ANGELO DUNDEE
(while tying)
He's right.

Dundee turns away to tear two strips of tape while Cassius and Malcolm face into a corner. Sarria throws a towel over Cassius' shoulders. Arms bent, head down, a true believer, he silently stands in prayer, bowing to the east with Malcolm. During this, Dundee starts collecting his cut gear on table.

MALCOLM X
It's a crusade in modern times. And television is beaming it off Telstar to the whole world. So Allah has brought this about for a reason...
(time to leave)
Salaam alaikum, my brother...

And as he goes, leaving us, not Cassius, incomplete, Cassius returns to Dundee, who ties gloves and puts tape over the knot. The Inspector signs that, too.

INT. A CORRIDOR, CASSIUS – NIGHT

A door slams open. Cassius comes along the hallway, his entourage surrounding him. Three large middle-aged white officials accompany him, too. His face is set in stone. White towels are draped over his head onto his shoulders. Bundini chirps in his ear. Dundee, like a plumber, carrying the tools of his trade...a bucket, his swabs and Vaseline. And they seem distant to Cassius. They reach the end of the corridor, and against the wall stand three or four older bad cigar guys. A curtain...the sounds from the arena drift into the hallway. Cassius is on his toes now, dancing, dancing. And as if being drawn by a force we can't see, he just goes...his entourage, as if holding on, carried along by him...

INT. THE MIAMI CONVENTION CENTER – NIGHT

He comes into the hall...there are shouts, some scattered applause, some booing, growing; and the sound moves through the arena...the sounds of expectations, ridicule, potential violence. But past the faces and the press, what's arrested Cassius' attention and makes him oblivious in his solitude to all else is the bright 20-by-20-foot place he wants to be most in all the world: the ring.

INT. THE RING - CASSIUS - NIGHT

is struck by the brilliance. Illuminated, ready to go...dancing...warming up. Counter to an expectation of anxiety, Cassius can't wait to get this on. Other sounds happen...irrelevant to him... and now the distant sound of Liston coming into the ring...his bulked-up presence, the roar he inspires, somewhere over there. And all of a sudden, Cassius turns to face the angry man who wishes him death. Cassius rocks left and right, like a tough kid on a corner ready to rumble. The hysteria act is gone; so is the boasting. Instead, there is only Cassius' stare. The effect is enigmatic: what is going on here? A Referee, like a distant bird, says something we don't hear...

In the corner, his feet float, waiting. There's the BELL for ROUND ONE.

INT. RING - ROUND ONE - WIDE

It starts.

LISTON

right away throws a left that misses and attacks Cassius, throwing seven more that Cassius with extreme, awkward caution evades.

He is fearful of the monster whose punches he has yet to feel. Nevertheless, he does his job: measure Liston's range and speed. Then, a body shot catches him above the heart. Cassius feels the real power of Liston. It could stop your heart's beating. He survives. Then...

CASSIUS

throws his long left jab. It keeps Liston at a set distance. He has Liston's range, now, and he dances away from Liston's charges. Then, halfway through the round, Cassius' eyes have hunted out an opportunity, and he throws his first combination with a few hard shots that, to Liston's surprise, rock Liston's head back. And, then, Cassius easily evades...

LISTON'S

furious big misses to the left and right.

CASSIUS

keeps tagging Liston with his long left. And, now, infuriates Liston even more by merely walking away from Liston's big misses, provoking even wilder and more inaccurate Liston assaults. (We're aware that any Liston shot could knock out Cassius if it connected.) Then Cassius soaks up a couple of body shots, mostly flicks his jab, slides, dances, clinches, circles away...UNTIL....

AT THE END OF THE ROUND

Cassius launches a second combination, slams a couple of big lefts Liston's way that rock his head back two times. Liston's so furious, he flips, charging Cassius, who hits and ducks at the same time. The BELL RINGS THREE TIMES before they stop.

CLAY'S CORNER - CASSIUS

breathes hard. Dundee works. Cassius says something we can't hear.

> CASSIUS
> He was supposed to kill me.
> Well, I'm still alive.

Angelo is talking to Clay a mile a minute, while Clay MUGS an open mouth...to the press, ridiculing their accusation he was all talk. It's clear he controlled Round One to everyone's surprise.

THE BELL. INT. RING, ROUND TWO - CASSIUS + LISTON

We see press with typewriters, ribbon, microphones, note pads; massive TV cameras hang on platforms over two of the corners. It's a desultory, lower-key version of Round One. And...

BIRD'S NEST TV CAMERA + MEDIA

Coverage segues to Liston, who throws and misses a few lefts. Cassius tags him with a few rights.

THE BELL. CASSIUS

literally ambles into the corner.

SONNY'S CORNER: HIS TWO TRAINERS

Liston's getting a lot of strident advice. THE BELL.

INT. RING, ROUND THREE

LISTON'S LEFT

comes in like a freight train. Cassius merely leans away to avoid Liston, circles and now snaps off a flurry and OPENS A CUT UNDER SONNY'S LEFT EYE. Then, he splits out of there.

> ANNOUNCER
> (at ringside, on radio)
> He's opened a cut on Liston.
> Liston's never been cut!

And Cassius, seizing opportunity, hits Liston with more combinations. If Cassius won Round One, probably but not certainly won Round Two, he now demonstrates he OWNS Round Three. It's a symphony of classical Cassius Clay footwork, flicked jabs that confuse, and, then, hard-hitting combinations that rock the presumably immovable Liston. No one told Sonny that Cassius could hit. And, at 210 pounds, he hits HARD. Liston, angered, panicked, knows he's losing and goes after Cassius and misses wildly as the BELL ends Round Three...

INT. CLAY'S CORNER - CLAY

stands a moment before he sits.

EXTREMELY CLOSE: CASSIUS CLAY

breathing heavily, ignoring the stool and Dundee and Bundini, looks around. THIS IS WHAT IT'S LIKE TO BE 22, TO BE CASSIUS CLAY, TO BE ON TOP OF YOUR GAME AND TO BE ABOUT TO OWN THE WORLD. He looks over his crowd. Only then, turns and sits...

> CASSIUS
> (to Dundee)
> He's nothin' to me...

The genius of Cassius...

> CASSIUS (Cont'd)
> And he knows it...

INT. LISTON'S CORNER - CORNERMAN

slips a vial of some medicant from his pocket and rubs it into Liston's shoulder.

INT. RING - ROUND FOUR

The BELL RINGS. Clay peppers Liston with jabs. Liston pokes his left at Cassius, trying to reach him. They feint, circle. Liston gets his left into Cassius' face. It's more a poke than a shot.

CLOSE: CASSIUS

blinks back something...we're not sure what. It seems to go away. Then it's back. The fight continues...

WIDER: CASSIUS

dominating. They clinch. They break. This time Cassius violently blinks his eyes! Something's wrong!

> CASSIUS
> ...my eyes!

A knife-like pain. He can't see. He's getting beaten up. He's in trouble. The BELL.

INT. RING, CASSIUS' CORNER - CASSIUS

sits.

CASSIUS
(shouting)
My eyes! I can't see...somethin'
in my eyes!

Dundee feverishly washes water to get
the irritant out of Cassius' eyes.

INT. ARENA

A buzzer sounds, warning the bell's
coming for Round Five. Now Cassius
stands, saying...

CASSIUS
(his gloves)
Cut 'em off! Cut 'em! I'm blind.

The BELL. Dundee's still in the ring.

ANGELO DUNDEE
No. You quit, it's over! Get out
there. Be a yardstick. This is the
big one, daddy. Get out there and
run!

He literally pushes Cassius into the ring.

INT. RING - ROUND FIVE - LISTON

rushes Clay. He knows this is his
chance. Cassius tries to tie Liston up
by holding onto the back of his neck,
but Liston pounds left and right
hooks. If anybody wondered if Clay
could take punishment, this answers
that. WHAM—WHAM—WHAM—WHAM—
WHAM...five huge hooks.

Liston is desperate to end it while
Cassius is in trouble. Haymaker after
haymaker; some connect, others are
blocked but knock Clay sideways. Clay,
still blind, keeps backing and dancing.

CLOSER: CASSIUS' EYES

With a minute left, now, he sees better.
Liston throws him into a corner, still
trying to put him away. But, he can't,
and Liston's energy seems to deflate
once he knows that. The BELL.

INT. RING, CASSIUS' CORNER - CASSIUS'

eyes are clear. In 60 seconds he recov-
ers his energy. He's ready. BELL.

INT. RING - ROUND SIX - CASSIUS

can't wait to get out. He shuffles. He
circles. He fires combinations. In the
early rounds, provoked by Cassius,
Liston's anger caused him to abandon
his fight plan. Now, having been proven
futile, Liston's confidence is gone. He's
left with nothing. Psychologically and
athletically, Liston is defeated. The
BELL. Liston's eyes contemplate the inev-
itable: face nine more rounds of this.

INT. RING, CASSIUS' CORNER – BETWEEN
ROUNDS – AS CASSIUS

waits for the seventh-round bell.

HOWARD COSELL
(doing color radio commentary
with Les Keiter's blow-by-blow)
...Clay, a round ago, looked like he'd
about had it, but in round six...

Then Cassius, knowing before anybody
else, suddenly rises as if on wings.
Both arms are in the air...followed by
a roar from the crowd...

HOWARD COSELL (Cont'd)
(realizing, screaming)
Sonny Liston is not coming out!
Wait a minute! Wait a minute!
Sonny Liston is not coming out!

And we can see Liston still sitting on
his stool in his corner, spitting out his
mouthpiece.

HOWARD COSELL (Cont'd)
The winner...and the new
heavyweight champion of
the world is Cassius Clay!

Cassius jumps onto the ropes in the
corner, rails the crowd:

CASSIUS
I upset the world! I am the
greatest! I am the greatest!

All hell breaks loose...

CASSIUS (Cont'd)
(to press)
Eat your words! Eat your words!

Howard Cosell, the first to climb into
the ring, is on him...

HOWARD COSELL
What made him so easy for you?

CASSIUS
I told you. Didn't I tell you?

Bundini gives him a comb. Cassius
combing his hair.

HOWARD COSELL
Was there any single point you
knew you had him?

And he sees Malcolm leaving his
seat...they look at each other. Malcolm's huge smile.

CASSIUS
I had him in the first round.
'Cause I'm the greatest!
(and seeing at ringside,
calling him up)

Sam... Hey, Sam! Let him up.

And Sam Cooke climbs into the ring.

CASSIUS (Cont'd)
I am the greatest! And he the
greatest rock 'n' roll singer.
Sam Cooke! I want everybody
to bear witness.
(they embrace)
I shook up the world! Don't have
a mark on me! I was burning. I
was blind. I'm the prettiest thing
that ever lived. I shook up the
world! I shook up the world!

As Sam Cooke embraces Cassius...

INT. ELIJAH MUHAMMAD'S HOUSE, LIVING
ROOM - WIDE - NIGHT

A small older man with fine features,
ELIJAH MUHAMMAD, THE MESSEN-
GER, sits on plastic-covered white fur-
niture in his expensive living room.
With him is an expressionless man
who, literally, never smiles, in a tai-
lored dark suit. He's JOSEPH 13X. As
Elijah Muhammad, the head of the
Nation of Islam, contemplates Cassius'
victory—like everyone else in
America, he's surprised.

INT. THE MIAMI BEACH CONVENTION CENTER -
PAY PHONE - NIGHT

GORDON DAVIDSON is from the Louisville Sponsoring Group, standing in
the chaos with another partner and
Odessa and Cassius, Sr....

GORDON DAVIDSON
...I don't care what should have
been ordered! We need a victory
party right now.
(pause)
I got national press, the family,
the champ, all kinds of folks...
(beat)
250 to 300. Yes.

INT. THE SIR JOHN NIGHTCLUB - SAM COOKE -
NIGHT

singing "Feel It." It's packed with elat-
ed people. Outside, celebrations spill
out onto the streets...cars honking...

EXT./INT. HAMPTON HOUSE VILLAS - CLOSE ON
COOKE AS HE CROSSES - NIGHT

through the club, with lots of party-
goers, picks up Chesterfields from the
cigarette girl and goes out by pool,
around which we see women at tables
in cocktail dresses and good-looking
men. Most of the rooms' doors are
wide open, couples drinking, celebrat-
ing...radios playing out into the
Floridian night.

INT. THE BALLROOM, THE RONEY PLAZA
HOTEL - GORDON DAVIDSON - NIGHT

and others of the Louisville Sponsoring
Group in a crowd of predominantly
white people, drinking free drinks at
the hastily arranged victory party,
wait. Sportswriters...Jimmy Cannon,
Red Smith. Cassius, Sr. is there. They
all wait. No sign of Cassius. "Where's
your boy?" A young New York Times
sportswriter, ROBERT LIPSYTE, is
there as well. He looks like he doesn't
belong...his clothes are only perfunc-
torily conventional, and he's a generation younger.

INT. HAMPTON HOUSE HOTEL ROOM - SAM
COOKE - NIGHT

enters and closes the door and greets
Malcolm X, in a white shirt, no tie,
and Cassius, eating ice cream in a pool
of light from the TV. Malcolm's wife,
Betty Shabazz, comes out of the kitchenette. A little girl runs from the
bathroom back to Cassius. The girl
plops into his lap with much familiarity, so we understand Cassius is family and has been for a while. He's not
at the party at the Fontainebleau or
the Roney Plaza. It says Cassius'
sense of himself is more about what's
next than what he did tonight.

GIRL
Why's he so scared?

MALCOLM X
Man, look at that guy run!

Cassius feeds the girl some ice cream.

CASSIUS
The Mummy! "I can't get away
from the mummy!" Yeah, but
that mummy too slow to catch
anybody.

SAM COOKE
Hey! The mummy always gets
his man...

CASSIUS
No, he don't!
(to kid)
Now, don't believe that stuff
on television...

Laughter from the outside. Cassius
looks. He's not drawn to all the party-
ing. Malcolm takes a picture with his
Contax. Through the door enters Jim
Brown. Jim embraces Malcolm and
Betty, Sam Cooke, and congratulates the
new champ and helps himself to food.

INT. THE HAMPTON HOUSE HOTEL ROOM, 1964 -
NIGHT, LATER

The room's near dark. Soft sounds
from outside. A laugh. A snatch of
music. Malcolm's children are asleep
on a cot. And we see Cassius has fall-
en asleep on the sofa. A bedsheet is
over him. Malcolm and Betty, sitting at
the table in the kitchenette, quietly
talking...an intimate laugh...partners.
And as Cassius, the new heavyweight
champion of the world, spends the
first night of his reign asleep at
"home" with this family...

EXT. 125TH STREET + 7TH AVENUE - CASSIUS,
MALCOLM + A CRUSH OF PEOPLE (NEW YORK,
1964) - DAY

Suddenly we're in Harlem. The streets
are jammed. Making them crazy, caus-
ing a riot, coming down the sidewalk,
looking like a rock-and-roll star in a
black leather jacket, is CASSIUS CLAY
and in an overcoat and hat, MALCOLM
X. They OWN this day on 125th Street.

EXT. MICHAUX BOOK SHOP - PEOPLE - DAY

engulf them. People are their army.
The sea of people press close to their
heroes...reaching out to touch the
champ, share a joke, laugh. A girl runs
up to hug Cassius and runs off. We
catch a glimpse on the periphery of
Joseph 13X. Seven or eight reporters,
black and white, and still photographers
and Bingham, half with Cassius, half
photographer in privileged position.

A REPORTER
The people look to you. Do you
plan on being a people's champ,
like Joe Louis?

CASSIUS
(tentative)
Yeah. I going to be a people's
champ...
(beat)
But not like Joe Louis, exactly...

A REPORTER
(starts)
Mr. Clay...?

And Cassius drops it on them...

CASSIUS
And I'm not Clay. Clay's the
name of the people who owned
my ancestors. I don't want to be
called after that slave name no
more. So I'm "X." Cassius X. And
I'm a member of the Nation of
Islam. The Honorable Elijah
Muhammad is my spiritual
guide. Malcolm X is my mentor.

This is hard news!

REPORTERS
(All at once)
You a card-carrying member?
Aren't Black Muslims a hate
group?

CASSIUS
(droll)
"Card-carrying"...? Don't need no
"card." You got a Christian card?
750 million people believe in
Islam. I'm one of them.

ANOTHER REPORTER (O.S.)
Minister Malcolm...what about
the reports of a split between
you and Elijah Muhammad?

JOSEPH 13X: we read his face listening to Malcolm.

MALCOLM X
This is the champ's time. And I'm
here as a friend to celebrate his
victory. So I got nothing you
want...

CASSIUS
I'm going to be a people's champion. But I don't have to be the
way you want me to be. I'm
gonna be what I want. And I'm
free to think any way I want...

And, as he goes on, the crowd knows
neither Cassius nor Malcolm will ever
turn their backs on them.

EXT. THE HOTEL THERESA - MALCOLM - NIGHT

enters into the street with his Bodyguard and looks up to a top-floor window in which he sees a light is still on
at 4 a.m.

INT. THE HOTEL THERESA, CASSIUS' ROOM -
CASSIUS - BEFORE DAWN

asleep with the television on. There's
a knock on the door. Barely awake, he
gets up to answer it. It's Malcolm. Still
in his familiar hat and overcoat. He
hasn't slept...

MALCOLM X
I was leaving, saw the light
on...how come you're up?

CASSIUS
(mumbles, half-asleep)
...watchin' a show on
termites...they knockin' down
this house, here.

He goes back to lay on the bed. Malcolm looks out the window...the wet
streets at night.

MALCOLM X
I been invited to speak at Ibadan

University in Nigeria. C'mon with me?

CASSIUS
Six million in your house and you don't know it. Where?

MALCOLM X
Africa. You been there?

CASSIUS
Africa? No. Only Rome. Yeah, man, let's go!

MALCOLM X
Nkrumah stayed with me when he was a student in New York, so we'll stop in Ghana...

CASSIUS
When we leaving?

MALCOLM X
Next Thursday.

Malcolm's distracted. He fingers his glasses.

CASSIUS
(sees)
What is it?

MALCOLM X
You ever been so angry...have you ever been so angry that you'd explode?

CASSIUS
(after a beat)
Tore out a picture of Emmett Till when I was little. Couldn't take my eyes to it...couldn't look at it. Barbwire around his neck to a 75-pound cotton-gin fan. Took out his eye. The cruelty to it...I couldn't look at it...couldn't throw it away.

MALCOLM X
What else?

CASSIUS
I thought, "What I do wrong to be so low that people could do that to people like me?" It made me feel ashamed. And that makes no sense. But that's what it was.

MALCOLM X
...when I heard about the four girls bombed in the 16th Street Church in Birmingham?
(beat)
The prohibitions of the Honorable Elijah Muhammad prevented me from speaking my voice in action. Because Birmingham was part of the civil rights movement, begging for a place at the white man's

table...But dead children...are dead children. So the anger I felt, I had to contain. I locked that down! So tight my muscles seized. I lost control over the right side of my body. Leg didn't work...right arm didn't work. "I'm having a stroke," I thought. I had to hold it in 'cause I wanted, all I wanted was to BREAK SOMETHING! Break a part...any part of this system. Because you are so provoked as a human being. In your spirit. In your heart...At the death of children. But I COULD DO...nothing.

Cassius is quiet.

MALCOLM X *(Cont'd)*
(putting his glasses back on)
Everyone knows...Now I'm advocating more direct political action involvement with the international struggle...So Elijah Muhammad has suspended me as a Minister in the Nation of Islam for 90 days.

CASSIUS
You can fix that...

MALCOLM X
I don't know. I will try when we get back. Until then I will live each day as if I am already dead.

That statement surprises Cassius, but he says nothing. Malcolm X stands by the window and watches the day begin in Harlem.

INT. ELIJAH MUHAMMAD'S HOUSE, CHICAGO, 1964 - JOSEPH 13X - DAY

approaches Cassius in a suit and tie and beckons him into a living room in which sits Elijah Muhammad on a plastic-covered white sofa. Cassius is at his most deferential, awed at being in this man's presence. Elijah's power is the inverse of his size. He's short and delicate-featured. He motions for Cassius to sit beside him. Joseph 13X sits across the room with two men.

ELIJAH MUHAMMAD
Only after long service and high merit in the spiritual and physical rebirth of Afro-American people... is one granted an original name. But you are special. A world champion. So there is a gift I wish to give you. From this day forward you will be known as Muhammad Ali...which means "one worthy of praise," and Ali means "most high."

CASSIUS
(a beat, sounding it)
Muhammad Ali.
(humble)
"Worthy of praise..." Thank you!

And he's genuinely moved. As Elijah Muhammad puts his small hands in Muhammad Ali's hands...giving him his blessings...

ELIJAH MUHAMMAD
(cautioning)
Be very careful what you say... your words reflect on the Nation of Islam, now.

CASSIUS
Yes, sir.

ELIJAH MUHAMMAD
(after a beat)
Up until now, I have entrusted your spiritual development to Brother Malcolm.
(beat)
I do not feel this is a wise course anymore.

Extremely emotional about Malcolm, tears come to Elijah Muhammad's eyes. Joseph 13X observes in the background. Cassius is taken by surprise at "The Messenger"'s display...

ELIJAH MUHAMMAD *(Cont'd)*
Malcolm has gone off into the secular world and does not measure his words. I have decided to give you, as your guide, my very own son, Herbert Muhammad.

And he looks across the room...a roly-poly man wearing a bow tie...HERBERT MUHAMMAD. He has a habit of nervously straightening his shirt. A seemingly mild, pleasant man, he is without self-definition. Below this avuncular surface, he defines himself by quietly desiring and acquiring what is others'.

ELIJAH MUHAMMAD *(Cont'd)*
Herbert will supervise all of your spiritual and material needs.

CASSIUS
(not a thought)
This is a great honor, Messenger...

Elijah gives a subtle look and Herbert retreats to where he came from, sitting back on the couch by Joseph 13X...

EXT. THE CLAY HOUSE, LOUISVILLE, 1964 – EVENING

We've entered mid-scene.

> **CASSIUS CLAY, SR.**
> Why you want to change?

> **A NEIGHBOR** (V.O.)
> (to Ali)
> Could we get a picture with you?
> (to Cassius, Sr.)
> You mind, Mr. Clay?

A neighboring family coming to stand beside Ali. Cassius, Sr. steps aside.

CASSIUS CLAY, SR., a sport, a flamboyant man, is impatient. Inside, Odessa Clay and brother, Rudy, are talking.

> **CASSIUS CLAY, SR.**
> What's wrong with the lawyers and managers you got?

> **A NEIGHBOR**
> One more.
> (click)
> Thank you.

> **CASSIUS CLAY, SR.**
> Yeah, yeah...

They leave.

> **CASSIUS CLAY, SR.** (Cont'd)
> You got...I got you the best white men I could find. Right here in L'ville...

> **ALI**
> When the contract run out. I want black lawyers and managers. Chauncey Eskridge on North La Salle Street...

> **CASSIUS CLAY, SR.**
> (angrily)
> They saved you from the gangsters, from the jackals and the hyenas of boxing. Never cheated you. Protect you with a trust fund...

> **ALI**
> I don't need no "protectin'" from myself. Why I need protecting from myself by them...?

> **CASSIUS CLAY, SR.**
> And now I got to go tell them, "Piss off. Cassius don't want you around no more."

> **ALI**
> I ain't one of their thoroughbreds! Or their charity things. "Let's do somethin' for that well-behaved colored boy, Cassius." I ain't well-behaved nothing! I am a man.

The light starts to go...porch lights starting to come on...

> **ALI** (Cont'd)
> And I am not Cassius. I changed my name. I am Muhammad Ali, now.

> **CASSIUS CLAY, SR.**
> You what?

> **ALI**
> That's right.

> **CASSIUS CLAY, SR.**
> (stunned)
> What? What's wrong with...our name, my name...? We're...we made you. We...

> **ALI**
> No one "made me"...

> **CASSIUS CLAY, SR.**
> No bow-tie-wearin', Arab-talkin' nigger gonna change that...

> **ALI**
> (anybody's son)
> I made me.
> (adamant)
> No one's in that ring but me!

> **CASSIUS CLAY, SR.**
> You don't know who you are...

> **ALI**
> I know who I'm not...I'm not drinkin'! Goin' back on my wife! I am not prayin' to no blue-eyed, blonde-haired Jesus. I ain't...

> **CASSIUS CLAY, SR.**
> Paintin' blue-eyed, blonde-haired Jesuses and signs on cars is what put steak and vegetables in you, clothes on you...

> **ODESSA CLAY**
> ...dinner!

And we realize it has gotten too dark to see...

> **CASSIUS CLAY, SR.**
> (cold)
> Go ahead!

Bitter silences.

> **CASSIUS CLAY, SR.** (Cont'd)
> Go ahead.

Cassius, Sr. walks off...his back arched too straight, trying to hold his pride together.

> **ODESSA CLAY**
> You didn't get it from me...your words, your sense of humor, what makes you angry, what makes you a fighter. You got that from your daddy...

> **ALI**
> You saying I'm just like him?

> **ODESSA CLAY**
> I'm saying, if he was your age today, he'd do the same as you. And he knows that.

And Odessa goes back inside.

INT. MALCOLM'S HOUSE, KITCHEN (QUEENS, NEW YORK), 1964 – NIGHT

We see Malcolm at work at the kitchen table. It's cluttered and small. The telephone rings...

> **ONE OF HIS CHILDREN** (Over)
> Daddy...For you...

Malcolm gets it.

> **JOSEPH 13X** (V.O.)
> Brother Malcolm...

> **MALCOLM X**
> What is it, Joseph?

> **JOSEPH 13X** (V.O.)
> The Honorable Elijah Muhammad has given the Muslim name, Muhammad Ali, to Cassius X. Herbert Muhammad's been placed in charge of his training, instead of you.
> (and ultimately)
> Muhammad Ali will not be traveling with you to Africa.

Malcolm's still. He's been co-opted.

> **JOSEPH 13X** (V.O.) (Cont'd)
> The Honorable Elijah Muhammad has asked me to inform you your suspension has been extended indefinitely.

Joseph 13X hangs up. Malcolm quietly closes the door. Malcolm dials a number. No answer.

Betty has come in. They exchange a look.

> **BETTY SHABAZZ**
> (concerned for her husband)
> Malcolm?

> **MALCOLM X**
> (after a beat, disconsolate)

Cassius won't be coming to Africa...not with me.

She puts her hand on Malcolm's shoulder.

BETTY SHABAZZ
Go anyway. Don't put it off. It's not safe here.

ONE OF HIS CHILDREN (Over)
(calling)
Mommy...the bath's ready...

CUT TO:

INT. GHANA AIR DC-8 COCKPIT - ALI - NIGHT

in first class on a "Ghana Airlines" flight to Africa. Close by is Herbert Muhammad. Howard Bingham and Ali's brother, Rudy, are across the aisle from him, asleep...The plane bumps in choppy air.

Muhammad, unable to sleep, a nervous flyer, gets up. He wanders up the aisle to the front of the plane. A Stewardess comes out of the cockpit. Muhammad slows, startled by the pilots. Both pilot and copilot are black.

ALI
(joking)
Hey, man, where they put the real pilot? What you doin' up here?

PILOT
(not understanding; British accent)
I am...the pilot. He's the copilot...
(moves map case)
Here, Mr. Clay, sit down...

ALI
No, man, I meant...in L'ville, when I growed up, they barely let black folks drive buses.

Ali looks out the window...a new day dawns over the land. Then Bingham shows up over Ali's shoulder. They all pose, facing the rear of the cockpit. Then, the Pilot points to the coast below them and the sunrise...

THE PILOT
Here we are. Cote d'Ivoire...Africa.

CUT TO:

EXT. BUILDING IN CAIRO - CABLE - DAY (EGYPT)

snakes out a building. CAM FOLLOWS IT and we HEAR...

BETTY SHABAZZ (V.O.)
We should think of a name, Malcolm...

INT. CAIRO BUILDING - WIDE: HALLWAY - DAY

MARLIN THOMAS—paunchy, grey, late 40's—walks up the stairs carrying take-out food.

MALCOLM X (V.O.)
How about Gamilah or Khalilah?

INT. CAIRO EMPTY APARTMENT - MARLIN THOMAS - DAY

crosses to ANOTHER AMERICAN wearing headphones in the glassed-in balcony where the CABLE connects to a portable tape recorder.

MARLIN THOMAS
(eating)
Anything?

THE MAN
...on the phone with his wife. She's having a hard time sleeping...baby's kicking a lot...

MARLIN THOMAS
Motor Pool, here, have a Chevy parts catalogue...?

As the CIA monitors Malcolm X...

CUT TO:

EXT. INDEPENDENCE SQUARE, ACCRA - ALI - DAY (GHANA)

in a Mercedes convertible. It's a monumental expression of the force for the independence of black Africa. Accra is a wonder to Ali. A Third World showplace, in 1964 Ghana is alive with the optimism of emerging Africa. Infrastructure and real estate are well-managed. Under Nkrumah, the city is in a frenzy of building public housing...

ALI
in the three-car caravan, passes under the huge triumphal arch with its giant black star on the top. Thousands line the route to see the heavyweight champion and cheer him. For Ali it's another kind of parade...

ALI'S POV: GHANAIANS

They're stockbrokers and street cleaners, salesmen and secretaries, hotel managers and military officers...All is a contrast to the exclusion by de facto apartheid of the middle America of Ali's experience. They all cheer his caravan as it passes.

CUT TO:

EXT. THE AMBASSADOR HOTEL, ACCRA - MERCEDES - LATE AFTERNOON (GHANA)

arrives with Ali and entourage. It's a

modern hotel. Meanwhile, a different group are about to depart in limos. One among them, a tall Man in a dashiki and sunglasses and carrying a walking stick, separates. He sees Ali. So does the woman next to him. She is the poet Maya Angelou.

MALCOLM X
(shouts)
Brother Muhammad...

Taking off his shades, we realize it's Malcolm X. He wears a goatee, now. Ali turns, sees him. Total surprise.

ALI
Hey, man!!!

They embrace. Ali greets him like the old friend he is. Maya and the Chinese diplomat wait a few steps removed.

ALI (Cont'd)
How you doin'? What's up, brother? I knew you were here... didn't think you were still here...

MALCOLM X
And I heard you were coming.

ALI
We just got here now...
(words rush out)
And, maaan, the brothers were flyin' a DC 8. Flippin' switches; navigatin', filing flight plans, talkin' French...

And they remember how much they like each other.

ALI (Cont'd)
Where you goin'?

MALCOLM X
When...uh, Liberia. When you fighting Liston?

ALI
November.

MALCOLM X
This is Maya Angelou and Ambassador Huang Ha. Amando Gonzalez is from Cuba. Taher Kaid is the Ambassador from Algeria.

Ali waves. They keep their distance.

ALI
Man, where should I go? We're planning on Egypt.

MALCOLM X
Algeria. See Ben Bella...
(beat)
Go to Mecca, Medina. I just came

back. Made my seven circuits around the Kaaba, prayed at sunrise...There were two million people...pilgrims from all over. Dressed all the same, high and low, the same. Blonde-haired, blue-eyed Muslims. Arabs.
(off Ali's look of surprise)
Blacks. Yeah. All of them, Muslims praying together.

INT. AMBASSADOR HOTEL ROOM – MARLIN THOMAS – DAY

who was surveilling Malcolm X in Cairo is here, too. Right now he picks up the phone. REVEAL at the window an African Man and another American with binoculars.

BRADLEY (V.O.)
Hello...?

MARLIN THOMAS
It's Marlin. You'll never guess who Malcolm ran into...

CUT TO:

INT. LEOPOLDVILLE SCHOOL – CLASSROOM – BRADLEY – DAY (CONGO)

BRADLEY
(in French; into phone)
Un moment...

BRADLEY (Cont'd)
(English translation; into phone)
Hold on a second...

BRADLEY, an American in his late 30's who's balding and whose mouth is too wide, sits at the teacher's desk in an empty classroom. A heavyset American and two Black African Thugs with M-1 carbines are with him.

MOBUTU'S MILITARY AIDE
(in French)
Le Ministère de Défense vous remercie.

MOBUTU'S MILITARY AIDE (Cont'd)
(English translation)
The Defense Minister thanks you.

Uniformed MOBUTU'S MILITARY AIDE smiles and warmly shakes Bradley's hand. Bradley says "he's welcome" and signals to the Heavyset American. The American leads Mobutu's Military Aide somewhere. Meanwhile...

BRADLEY
(in French)
Il n'y a pas de quoi. Cela m'a fait grand plaisir. Faites-lui mes compliments.

BRADLEY (Cont'd)
(English translation)
It's nothing. Give him my compliments.

INT. LEOPOLDVILLE SCHOOL CORRIDOR – MOBUTU'S MILITARY AIDE FOLLOWS BRADLEY'S AMERICAN

to a sports court. Eight Uniformed

Soldiers are with them. In the sports court, on their knees, hands bound behind them, facing away from us, are six prisoners in business clothes. One is a woman. Guarding them are Bradley's Guards. Mobutu's Military Aide's soldiers take over the prisoners. Mobutu's Military Aide talks into a walkie-talkie. Meanwhile...

GEN. JOSEPH MOBUTU IN UNIFORM

listens to his walkie-talkie. He has distant eyes. He's heard what he needs and walks up a staircase and around a corner.

INT. LEOPOLDVILLE SCHOOL, SECOND CLASSROOM – MOBUTU

enters. He is the beneficiary of this routine military coup. Other uniformed officers at students' desks now stand and applaud. Mobutu will rename the Congo "Zaire" and we'll see him again later. Meanwhile in Ghana...

INT. AMBASSADOR HOTEL ROOM – MARLIN THOMAS – DAY

MARLIN THOMAS
Malcolm bumped into Cassius Clay. Muhammad Ali...whatever he calls himself...

BRADLEY
I thought that was all over. Is Clay going to support Malcolm's U.N. resolution?

MARLIN THOMAS
I don't know.

BRADLEY
Find out. We'll pick up on Malcolm in Liberia ourselves.

EXT. AMBASSADOR HOTEL – ALI + MALCOLM X

MALCOLM X
Drank from the well of Zem-Zem... And you should visit Cairo. I have friends there in...

Meanwhile...

ALI
(his thoughts)
...shouldn't have quarreled with the Honorable Elijah...

The rapport between them becomes fleeting. Ali's attention drifts away. He closes down...

ALI *(Cont'd)*
(to himself)
You shouldn't have...
(vocalized)

...quarreled with the honorable Elijah Muhammad...

MALCOLM X
What?

ALI
You shouldn't have quarreled with Elijah Muhammad.

And Ali separates. He turns away. Malcolm calls after him...

MALCOLM X
Brother Muhammad...

Ali won't turn back from his rejection of Malcolm. He shakes his head "no" and walks off.

MALCOLM X *(Cont'd)*
Brother Muhammad...!

INT. TIGER LOUNGE, CHICAGO – SHERI – NIGHT

sings "For Your Precious Love," and REVEAL: ALI + SONJI ROI dancing. We're back in Chicago. She's sexy and has a great smile and flashing eyes.

People leave Ali alone. One Fruit of Islam bodyguard is nearby, semi-conspicuous. In a booth is Herbert with a date, another FOI guard, and a businessman. Sonji, who is sexually overt and fun, is laminated to Ali. After a few bars...

ALI
Sonji...Sonji Roi...

SONJI
(laughs)
What you keep sayin' my name for?

ALI
'Cause I love it, girl. How long you been' workin' for Herbert?

SONJI
'Bout a year. I sell "Muhammad Speaks" over the phone...

ALI
What kind of name is that?

SONJI
My father named me after Sonja Henie.

ALI
What's your father do?

SONJI
He was shot in a poker game when I was two. He don't do nothin'. Sonja, on the other hand, was an ice skater, and my mother died when I was eleven.

ALI
So who raised you?

SONJI
Godparents, but I been on my own, doing my own thing...

ALI
Whatcha' doin' tomorrow? Go ridin' with me.

SONJI
No. I gotta work, you know.

ALI
I square it with Herbert. I got a record player in my car.

SONJI
A record player? C'mon. How come it don't skip?

ALI
Got springs and stuff.

SONJI
Herbert said you met The Beatles.

ALI
Yeah. Only one of 'em's smart...the one with the glasses.

SONJI
...he's my favorite.

ALI
People all screaming and fainting. I asked him, "This the way they act when you get big?"

SONJI
What he say?

ALI
He said, "Champ. The more real you get, the more unreal it gonna get."

SONJI
Wow...

After Sheri sings the first chorus...

ALI
Let's go...

SONJI
Yeah...

ALI
(crossing out)
Where you live?

SONJI
I'm takin' you there...

Herbert looks up from his booth, starts to ask where they're going...but they're gone. He turns back to the man he's talking to...

INT. SONJI'S APARTMENT – WINDOW – NIGHT (1964)

PULL BACK from being above Chicago in the winter at night to Ali and Sonji making love while Sheri's voice sings the second verse. To Ali's reactions...

ALI
I think I gonna keep you around forever, girl.

SONJI
(laughs)
Well, I'm not too busy right now, so...I'll think on it.

ALI
Herbert said you weren't a Muslim.

SONJI
Cover my hair? No make-up? Long dresses? Honey, please.
(beat)
Were you a virgin?

ALI
Why?

SONJI
(laughs)
'Cause you so "gone" off a little good time.

ALI
I'm no virgin...but I may as well be.
(beat)
I ain't jokin'! I always know when I know. See this face? I mean, you got a pretty face for a girl's face, but you ever seen somethin' as pretty as me? Now, you about five-feet-three...that's too small. But I overlook that, too, 'cause...

SONJI
(sarcastic)
Thank you so much.

ALI
...'cause of your spirit!

SONJI
My "spirit"...?

ALI
Yeah. 'Cause you too much fun!

SONJI
You serious?

She raises his head next to hers, looks in his eyes.

ALI
But you gotta be a Muslim.

SONJI
Huh? How you do that? Step over a broom...shazaam...you a Muslim?

She laughs. He rests his head on her stomach. He likes her irreverence...

ALI
Maaan, I ain't never been with a girl like you.

SONJI
Baby, maybe you ain't ever gonna be with any other.

They start making love again.

EXT./INT. 50TH ON THE LAKE MOTEL, COFFEE SHOP – ALI, HERBERT, BUNDINI + BINGHAM – DAY

HERBERT
What?

ALI
That's right. I wanna marry her.

HERBERT
You can't marry that girl! She was a date! Have some fun! She's not your wife! You don't marry this girl.
(puts contracts in front of him)
Sign there. Management papers. My father will kill me.

BUNDINI
True love!

Bundini cracks up. Ali signs without even glancing at the documents. Bingham notices this.

BINGHAM
Watch what you signing, Ali.

HERBERT
(to Bingham; sharp)
Nothing to do with you.

BINGHAM
You talkin' to me, or someone walk inna room, fat boy? Anything's to do with me I think's to d-d-do with me...I'm st-st-still a Christian.

ALI
(signs anyway)
And get me a kosher cook...lady

who cooks at Malcolm's temple. Put my brother on the payroll. 50g a year for drivin' and jivin'.

HERBERT
Lana Shabazz...

ALI
Yeah. How 'bout it, Howard? You be my official full-time photographer.

BINGHAM
I ain't goin' on your payroll. I like it freelance. Emphasis on "free."

As Ali signs the last of the contracts.

HERBERT
Muhammad. She's not...for you. When I met her, she was working at a cocktail lounge with a bunny tail on her backside.

BUNDINI
What were you doin' down at a cocktail lounge, Herbert? Sellin' "Muhammad Peeks"?

Ali and Bingham crack up...

HERBERT
(to Bundini)
Sober up and say something to this man, Bundini. You supposed to be his "inspiration."

BUNDINI
(looks at Ali; to Ali, serious)
I got to know about Sonji, Muhammad. She got a sister?
(as Ali laughs)

BINGHAM
You been s-s-saving it up, training, Champ. You can't unleash it on this girl all sudden. You may kill her! Maybe you should spread it around more before you tie it down.

ALI
No. Marriage is the cornerstone of Muslim life.

HERBERT
Sonji Roi is not a Muslim!

ALI
She gonna be a Muslim, now!
(flashes)
So fix it up, Herbert.

INT. FIFTH STREET GYM – ALI

past a speed bag onto Ali with Dundee + Sarria on the exercise table. They do NOT see, and we PASS them and other training boxers and MOVE IN to a portable B&W TV on top of a cabinet.

ON B&W TV: MALCOLM X + MARTIN LUTHER KING, JR.

exchange greetings and introductions as if in a first-time meeting, and King turns back to CAMERA.

MARTIN LUTHER KING, JR.
(mid-statement)
I fear if this bill is not passed...
(beat)
...our nation is in for a dark night of social disruption.

As an anchorman pontificates... IMAGE SUDDENLY BECOMES: FIVE DIFFERENT SURVEILLANCE ANGLES. King and Malcolm have no clue how extensive is the FBI Cointelpro surveillance and operations mounted against them. And the image of the two of them becomes...

INT. A COFFEE SHOP (WASHINGTON, D.C.) – THEIR PICTURE – SMILEY – DAY

on the front page of the Washington Post. REVEAL Joseph 13X sitting next to JOE SMILEY in a small Washington, D.C. coffee shop.

JOSEPH 13X
Why we meeting?

JOE SMILEY
The idea was...to...make...Malcolm smaller, you know? Diminished; obscure? Not to turn him into a messiah.
(the paper)
What I got, now, is Malcolm shoulder to shoulder with Martin Luther King.
(beat)
And Malcolm running all over the world getting Ben Bella and Nasser to denounce racism in the U.S. while we're competing over there with the Soviets.
(droll)
Not...a resounding success. We were better off before, with Malcolm INSIDE the Nation.
(beat)
So...We want you...to get Elijah Muhammad...to take Malcolm back.

Joseph 13X stares at him, slack-jawed. Incredulous. No reaction.

JOE SMILEY (Cont'd)
That's a joke. I'm kidding! You ever smile?

Joseph 13X doesn't say anything. He does not smile.

JOE SMILEY (Cont'd)
We're on a timetable. Malcolm's

pal, Quaison from Ghana, is introducing Malcolm's resolution to the General Assembly in Washington. That's in five weeks.

Joseph 13X oddly gets up, moving a stool over...

JOSEPH 13X
You got bad breath, man.

JOE SMILEY
Thyroid. I got a stab wound in 1961. They took it out. We gotta talk about this guy, too.

Smiley indicates the picture of Ali in "Muhammad Speaks" identifying him as a militant and a revolutionary.

JOSEPH 13X
When do I get my expenses reimbursed...dry cleaning lots of suits isn't free...

Off Ali's picture...it becomes...

INT. MIAMI HOTEL ROOM – ALI – NIGHT

enters, looking for Sonji. Bundini and Cassius Clay, Sr. were laughing about something else. They got quiet. Bundini has a large water glass in his hand; Sr., a highball glass.

ALI
(to Bundini)
What you drinkin'?

BUNDINI
What am I drinkin'? Water's what I'm drinkin', champ! I'm a natural man...

Ali goes to the bedroom door.

ALI
What's goin' on? We're late.

He's dressed for an occasion.

SONJI (V.O.)
I'm changing my damn clothes! You didn't like what I was wearin'!

As Ali re-enters the living room, there's a knock on the door..."Room Service..."

BUNDINI
Come on in...!
(sees)
What's that?

ROOM SERVICE
(with large glass)
What you wanted, isn't it... a water glass with vodka...?

BUNDINI
That was before...

ROOM SERVICE
Before what?

BUNDINI
Before you showed up...

And, now, Sonji comes out. This dress makes what she had been wearing look demure. Tight angora sweater and a miniskirt. She's Tina Turner 30 years ago.

SONJI
I fine runnin' around in all these cute short things for you. I submissive to you. But I ain't gonna be submissive to the Brother X's and what they think. They askin' me questions alla time anyway.

ALI
What questions?!

SONJI (V.O.)
About you and us, and I ain't tellin' 'em shit.

CASSIUS CLAY, SR.
(drunk)
Tell it like it is, sugar! They took my boy's name...and what they give him back? Bad style.

Ali takes her back into the bedroom and closes the door.

SONJI
I don't drink. I don't smoke. I converted to Islam for you and...

INT. BEDROOM - SONJI + ALI - NIGHT
SONJI
All except the dress! I ain't puttin' no bleached-out, double-ugly bedsheets on this body, honey! I'm normal!

He's furious. She smiles. He picks her up. She moans and her tongue darts in his ear and they're on the bed making out. And as CAMERA DRIFTS away we HEAR D.J. Daddio Daley's "Jazz Patio"...

INT. A NEW CAR (CHICAGO) - ALI - DAY
king of the city, cruising through the pristine winter air of Chicago...

DADDIO
(on radio)
Hey there, old, aware ones. And you, too, my fair ones...This is "Daddio's Jazz Patio." ON KBCA this fine day, which is A-okay...

Segues to...Brubeck's "Time Out," cruising...

INT. THE AUDUBON BALLROOM, HARLEM - REAR OF MALCOLM'S HEAD - DAY
center-punches the FRAME through the green-glazed terra-cotta hallway. He and his Bodyguard (#1) come to a door. Shedding his coat, he hesitates, and like a prizefighter gathering himself, he goes inside.

INT. ALI'S NEW CAR - ALI - DAY
at a light, waves to a cluster of girls waiting for a bus who recognize him, go nuts...listening to Brubeck...

INT. THE AUDUBON BALLROOM - MALCOLM - DAY
walks across the stage, aware of every little sound, every motion. He makes his way to the podium...peering beyond his glasses at the gathered. Bodyguard #1 goes to the side door instead of standing next to him...and Malcolm notices that...as he...

MALCOLM X
As-Salaam Alaikum...

THE GATHERED
Wa-Alaikum-Salaam...

And two young Black men, TALMADGE HAYER and NORMAN BUTLER immediately stand up in the back, jostling each other...

A YOUNG MAN
(shouts)
What you doin' in my pockets, man? Get your hand outta my pocket!

MALCOLM X
Hold it, hold it, brothers!
(pleading)
Let's be cool.

And the commotion in the back diverts Bodyguards #1 and #2 towards the rear, away from the stage and Malcolm, as...

THOMAS JOHNSON comes forward from a front row, his coat flapping open, revealing the 12-gauge sawed-off double-barrel shotgun coming up.

MALCOLM'S EYES
go to it. Settle on it. He knew it was coming, as...

JOHNSON, an indifferent expression on his face, FIRES one barrel at...

MALCOLM
...which rips through the lectern as if paper and SLAMS a dead-center into his chest a seven-inch ring. 12 pellets, each the size of .32 bullet. Seven destroy Malcolm's heart. Five shred his aorta and burrow into his spine. Malcolm's hands fly back, and he topples, crashing off empty chairs onto the floor.

UPSIDEDOWN ECU: MALCOLM'S FACE + PAST
...as life exhales from his mouth and his eyes go grey, dying, indifferent to Johnson emptying a second blast into him and the meaningless indignities of Hayer and Butler firing a .45 and a 9mm Luger at him.

INT. ALI'S CAR - RADIO - DAY
Dave Brubeck, loud...

INT. THE AUDUBON BALLROOM - STAGE - DAY
Chaos. Malcolm on the floor. Betty kneels over his body, desperately trying to breathe life into it. An Asian Woman, a disciple, holds up his head. Somebody shouts "Jesus, God!" But there is no God today...

INT. ALI'S CAR - ALI - DAY
stops short at a light because a man runs across the street.

CRAZY MAN
Ambushed!

LOUD Brubeck in 5/4 time. Ali can't hear.

CRAZY MAN (Cont'd)
From the bullet holes, black eagles flew! They screaming through the streets...

Ali rolls down the window.

ALI
What?

CRAZY MAN
(dazed)
...they killed Malcolm...they shot Malcolm.

"Daddio's Jazz Patio" is interrupted. Malcolm X has been killed. Ali pulls over...not really parking. The world stops. The South Side of Chicago goes still...people numb...a young Man sitting down on the curb, crying. An elegy...Sam Cooke's "A Change is Gonna Come..." plays. "I was born by a river in a little tent..." And as Ali sits in his car...he sees the face of Malcolm...the glasses...

ALI
(his thoughts)
You were the first...you walked me forward, my brother...you were the first...

He's overcome with a deep grief and a lack of confidence in the order of his world.

SAM COOKE
(sings)
"Been a long, long time comin', but a change gonna come, yes it is..."

INT. THE RING, ST. DOMINIC'S ARENA (LEWISTON, MAINE) - ALI - NIGHT

HOWARD COSELL
...the arena is surrounded by FBI, the stands are only half full, the promoter has taken out a million-dollar insurance policy due to Cassius Clay's membership in the militant and radical Black Muslims because of death threats. Oh, and by the way...Sonny Liston is here, too.

...sees Sonji enter in a sequined mini-dress, bouffant hair. She attracts attention and disapproval from Herbert. She sits next to Ali's parents at ringside amid the large, conservatively dressed Muslim contingent. He's angry at her presentation. She looks like a girl singer from a doo-wop group. He slips off his robe. Ali raises his gloves in Muslim prayer. Meanwhile: the BELL rings.

ALI

meets Liston, nails him with a straight right. Ali begins baiting him, dancing. Liston tries to cut off the ring, jabbing ineffectually. Ali lets Liston in, pulls back, then pivots on his right foot, throws a short right and RAMP INTO SLO-MO...to see Liston not see it coming.

The muscles of Ali's upper body contract and ripple in release after his short RIGHT catches Liston on the point of his chin. Liston drops to the canvas like a stone.

HOWARD COSELL (Cont'd)
Liston is down! Scarcely a minute into the first round, I can't believe it!

Sonji is up. For some reason, tears of worry stream, absurdly, from her eyes.

The IMAGE: Ali standing over Liston, fist cocked, bellowing:

ALI
Get up, sucker! Get up and fight! No one gonna believe this!

Liston tries to get up, rolls over. His left leg spasms. As the ref finally pushes Ali to a neutral corner.

HOWARD COSELL
It's over; it's over!

INT. MUHAMMAD'S DRESSING ROOM - NIGHT

Sarria, Bundini, Pacheco as Dundee cuts the tape off Muhammad's hands. And Sonji appears at the door...runs and embraces Ali.

SONJI
You okay?
(he's cold)
What's wrong?

ALI
Why you done up like that?

SONJI
I'm dyin' and...'cause this is how I dress! I dyin' for you out of worry...

ALI
"Worry"...?

SONJI
Yeah. And all you care about is if I look dull enough?

ALI
The world looks at me, girl! What if I straightened my hair, live in the white suburbs? How I am says something!

SONJI
(quiet; tough)
Well, sorry you don't like how I am...

EXT. HOLIDAY INN, BALCONY - ALI - NIGHT

enters up the stairs. Bundini's waiting for him as are Reporters, trying to ambush him. Lots of activity in the motel forecourt.

ALI
(to Bundini)
Where's Herbert?

Bundini indicates and Ali exits into Herbert's room. Beyond is the Holiday Inn marquee: "Clay vs. Liston II." A few letters droop.

EXT. HOLIDAY INN, HERBERT'S ROOM - ALI - NIGHT

ALI
What do I do...?

Ali, angry, stands in front of Herbert.

HERBERT
If you want, have no contact with her for ninety days. Then you make a public statement of divorce in the mosque, and Islamic law will be satisfied.

BUNDINI
"Satisfied?"...satisfaction is not makin' it with the woman who send you to the moon?

Cassius, Sr. bursts in. Bundini has Ali's championship belt over his shoulder.

BUNDINI (Cont'd)
Man, I'm the only normal person left around here and I'm a black Jew who can't read and is half drunk.

CASSIUS CLAY, SR.
I gotta talk to you.

Bundini and Herbert start to leave.

ALI
Please stay, Brother Herbert.

CASSIUS CLAY, SR.
He ain't your brother! Your brother taking your wife back to Chicago. She's crying like a widow.

ALI
I ain't dead!

CASSIUS CLAY, SR.
You might as well be. You don't remember your name or who you are.

Cassius, Sr. leaves the room.

INT. HOLIDAY INN, ALI'S MOTEL ROOM - HIGH ANGLE: ALI - NIGHT

enters. Stands at the dresser. Only his suitcase is there. She left her chartreuse blouse. He takes it and smells the scent of her cologne. He is torn with grief at the loss of her, curling into a ball on the bed, alone in the room.

INT. GREEN ROOM - ALI - DAY

getting made up by a good-looking ASIAN COSMETOLOGIST. An ASSISTANT DIRECTOR lounges against the wall with headset, reading the newspaper...

COSMETOLOGIST
You got the prettiest eyes...

ALI
Yeah?

BUNDINI
He so pretty, when you look up "pretty" in the dictionary, he too pretty to be in there.

She laughs and whispers something in Ali's ear, holding his hand where the others can't see it and slips her phone number to him. Meanwhile...a phone rings. Bundini answers while...

A.D.
(re: newspaper, to Ali)
...you gonna try for Germany?

ALI
Huh?

A.D.
You gonna try to get stationed in Germany?

ALI
What you talking about?

BUNDINI
Champ. It's Eskridge...

A.D.
(Ali didn't know)
They changed your classification.
(turns page)
It's in the paper...You're 1-A. You're gonna get drafted into the Army...

ALI
(takes phone)
You know about this?

CHAUNCEY ESKRIDGE *(V.O.)*
Yes. But I think the government's looking to negotiate a deal...

A.D.
(hears on headset)
Here we go...!

INT. A NEW YORK TELEVISION STUDIO, ABC – COSELL – DAY

"Wide World of Sports" is ON THE AIR. We've entered mid-broadcast.

ALI
...I flunk their draft board test. Now, without testing if I am "wiser" or "worser," they decide I can go into the Army.

HOWARD COSELL
Cassius, it is my opinion you...

ALI
(cuts in)
And I'm not Cassius Clay. That's a slave name. I'm a free man. I'm Muhammad Ali.

HOWARD COSELL
(stops, realizing)
You know, I apologize to you. On the air. Your name is Muhammad Ali. You have the right to be called whatever you want.

ALI
(stays angry)
You make a lot of mistakes for a so-called educated man. You really go to law school?

HOWARD COSELL
Yes, Muhammad. And to think I gave up a lucrative practice for the likes of you.

ALI
I'm the best thing that ever happened to you, Howard Cosell. Without me you be a tall white man with a microphone in his mouth.

HOWARD COSELL
(fast)
And without me...you'd be a mouth.

Ali lifts Howard's toupee.

HOWARD COSELL *(Cont'd)*
(into camera)
We'll be right back.

Laughter.

INT. ABC TELEVISION STUDIO, BACKSTAGE – ALI + COSELL – LATER

Ali pours three spoons of sugar in his coffee.

HOWARD COSELL
(sarcastic)
Have a little coffee with your sugar...?

ALI
Keep talking. You were saying something half-smart...

HOWARD COSELL
They want to make an example out of you.

ALI
Why? I'm no Stokely Carmichael, H. Rap Brown...

HOWARD COSELL
All they are is political. They tell people how they ought to be. But you are the HEAVYWEIGHT CHAMPION of the WORLD. You're important. And they don't like your militancy, your politics. So, they'll make an example out of you.

ALI
...of a good "Ne-gro," who do what he told?

HOWARD COSELL
Yes. Or, to demonstrate here is what happens to your ass if you don't...

He's screwed either way.

EXT./INT. THE UNITED STATES ARMED FORCES STATION, HOUSTON – LOBBY – CHAUNCEY ESKRIDGE – DAY

waits at the curb as Ali and Herbert pull up and get out of a car...move through the crowd...reporters shouting questions at him we don't hear, go up the steps, into the lobby, joining other recruits and M.P.'s.

CHAUNCEY ESKRIDGE
(quietly)
You do six weeks basic...you go into the Reserves...you don't go to Vietnam...you get to box...you even get to keep the money...

He gives Ali a piece of paper signed by the Justice Department, confirming the deal...

HERBERT
(lets him know)
The Messenger would not object if you joined under those terms.

ALI
I stay out of jail and I get to fight.

HERBERT
(nods)
All you have to do is accept the induction. And life goes on.

CHAUNCEY ESKRIDGE
They call your name. You say yes.

We're not sure what Ali will do.

INT. INDUCTION CENTER, HOUSTON – ALI – DAY

lined up with the twenty-five other inductees...being addressed by an Induction Officer, Naval LT. JEROME CLARIDGE...

LT. JEROME CLARIDGE
...and you will take one step forward as your name and service are called, and such a step will constitute your induction into the Armed Force indicated.

Lt. Claridge begins to read the names, and services...the young Men dutifully stepping forward. Ali expects his name to be called. Instead...

LT. JEROME CLARIDGE (cont'd)
Cassius Marcellus Clay.

It's quiet. Dead quiet. Ali's lips move. NO sound comes out. We anticipate him stepping forward...he doesn't.

LT. JEROME CLARIDGE (Cont'd)
Mr. Clay, I am required to inform you that refusal to accept a lawful induction order constitutes a felony under the Universal Military Training and Service Act, punishable by up to five years' imprisonment and a five-thousand-dollar fine. Do you understand?

ALI
(nods)
Yes.

TWO FBI AGENTS in suits have appeared.

LT. JEROME CLARIDGE
(repeats)
Cassius Marcellus Clay.

Ali doesn't move.

LT. JEROME CLARIDGE (Cont'd)
(a third time)
Cassius Marcellus Clay.

Herbert's dying. Ali "stands his ground..." and the die has been cast.

A MAN
(presenting badge)
Federal Bureau of Investigation. Mr. Clay, you're under arrest for refusing induction...

As they turn around and handcuff him.

EXT. HOLIDAY INN (HOUSTON) – ALI + ENTOURAGE – LATE AFTERNOON

approach from two vehicles. Rudy and SIX LARGE MUSLIMS escort Ali through the crowd of media trucks, reporters and conspicuous unmarked police cars and neighborhood people.

ALI

waves in Robert Lipsyte, the New York Times sportswriter in his late 20's we've seen before. He and Howard Bingham, waiting inside, know each other. They enter. The phone's already RINGING.

INT. HOLIDAY INN ROOM + BALCONY – ALI

on the phone, on a long extension, joined by Lipsyte and Howard Bingham, while Bundini keeps at bay

reporters at the front door. It all feels like a rock group in town for a concert.

ALI
(listens; to cam.)
Ask Chauncey Eskridge in Chicago. He's my lawyer. No. I'm out on bail.
(goes onto balcony {rear shot})
Yeah, I fight. I fight clean. I'm an athlete. Army's there to kill, kill, kill. My religion forbids that. No. I never shot anything in my life.
(turns)
Do I know where Vietnam is?
(wry; playing to Bingham)
Yeah. It's on TV...
(beat)
In southeast Asia? It there, too?
(beat)
That's a joke, man...!

Ali hangs up. The phone rings again.

ALI (Cont'd)
(frustrated)
What do I think about who? Vietcong?

Next is something Ali has not deduced. Ali perceives it intuitively and reflexively. As with other of his decisions, once made, he doesn't hesitate to speak them. And he won't waver. He says...

ALI (Cont'd)
Man, I ain't got no quarrel with them Vietcong.

It goes dead silent. Ali listens. Lipsyte is stunned. So's Howard.

ALI (Cont'd)
No Vietcong ever called me nigger.

BINGHAM
You know what you j-j-just said...?

He hangs up.

LIPSYTE
From Europe to China...every home in America...the world's gonna know what the heavyweight champion of the world said about the U.S. war...

ALI
So what?
(beat)
I ain't gonna be what anybody else want me to be. I'm not afraid to be what I want. And think how I want.

And that's the real Ali, right there.

INT. HOLIDAY INN, ALI'S SUITE – ALI – NIGHT

laying on the sofa. Dundee, Pacheco and Rudy have joined. There's the feeling the house is a bunker. Phones ring. Television is on. LIPSYTE, taking notes, watching Walter Cronkite on TV. He crosses to Ali. Dundee's on the phone.

LIPSYTE
(reading)
Nixon, the Republicans, Boxing Commission in New York, Cleveland and L.A.
(a foregone conclusion)
But you're also getting attacked as unpatriotic by the NAACP, Roy Wilkins, Jackie Robinson, the New York Times and Joe Louis...

The expression on Ali's face is blank, as if he's accepting a pounding: he knows what it is; it's not a surprise.

INT. GRANT PARK UNDERGROUND GARAGE – QUIET – NIGHT

A very low ceiling; we're in a green-lit cavern with a low ceiling. Chauncey Eskridge and Ali wait. Ali's in the backseat of a 1961 Lincoln. Two FOI Guards stationed at the distant ramps allow a Black Oldsmobile to pass.

BOB ARUM

a New York lawyer and promoter arrives and climbs out of the Oldsmobile. Ali opens the door...but doesn't get out...

ALI
(to Arum)
People are following me...

BOB ARUM
I got almost nowhere I can promote a fight for you. Plus, I think they're going to vacate you from the crown.

ALI
What?

BOB ARUM
Yeah. If you're convicted.

ALI
They gonna take away what no fighter in the world can?

BOB ARUM
And New York may revoke your boxing license.

CHAUNCEY ESKRIDGE
You sure you want to do all this?

(politics)
Your next three to four years
are every heavyweight's prime.
And there are few of those years...

ALI
What 'bout Terrell?

BOB ARUM
We'll know if we can fight
Terrell in Illinois this afternoon.
Terrell's running his mouth.
He said if you're called, you
should serve...

ALI
(angrily)
Motherfucker. He got a deferment
for bein' too tall, or havin' flat
feet. Why don't he serve for me?
Tellin' me what I should do...

BOB ARUM
(to Ali + Eskridge)
I got to get you some fights. Fast.

Ali's quiet, not really listening anymore...

INT. ILLINOIS BOXING COMMISSION - ALI - DAY

wearing a suit and a narrow tie at a
table in front of Daley machine appa-
ratchiks. A bald man, angrily:

COMMISSIONER
You understand we could take
away your license to fight Terrell
in Illinois?

ALI
Yes.

COMMISSIONER
Are you prepared to apologize?
About your unpatriotic remarks
that you made?

ALI
Apologize? No.

COMMISSIONER
You said that you were the
people's champion.

ALI
(angry)
Yes, sir!

COMMISSIONER
Do you think you're acting like
the people's champion...?!

ALI
Yes, sir. I am not going to apologize
to you. This isn't a courtroom.
And I don't have to sit here and
answer your questions.

He gets up and walks out on them. Eskridge and NOI men in black suits follow.

**INT. CHICAGO OFFICE BUILDING - ALI +
ENTOURAGE - DAY**

march through the lobby. Ali gives a
walking interview. He's angry. He won't
slow down.

ALI
I ain't draft dodgin'! I ain't goin'
to Canada. I ain't burnin' my
draft card. I ain't burnin' the
flag. I'm stayin' right here. And
you want to throw me in jail? Go
ahead. I'll do my time. I been in
jail four hundred years. I'll be in
jail four, five more. But I ain't
goin' ten thousand miles to help
murder and kill poor people for
you. 'Cause if I'm gonna die, I'll
die now, right here, fighting you.
If I wanna die. You my enemy,
not Vietcong or Chinese or
Japanese. You my opposer when I
want freedom. You my opposer
when I want justice. You my
opposer when I want equality.
You want me to go somewhere
for you, but you won't even stand
up for me in America, for my
rights and beliefs, you won't even
stand up for me here at home.

**INT. THE HOUSTON ASTRODOME -
CLOSE: TERRELL - DAY**

ERNIE TERRELL is taller than Ali. The
empty stadium has a scale and press
at one end. Girls in cowboy hats and
lone stars say we're in Texas. Ali is
distracted.

ERNIE TERRELL
(getting on scale)
Tell Clay he can get on after me.

ALI
What...?

ERNIE TERRELL
Get on the scale after...

ALI
(cuts in)
What you call me...?

Terrell wrongly thinks there's psychological value in provoking Ali.

ERNIE TERRELL
Only thing I knows you as:
Cassius Clay!

ALI
(infuriated)
Announce it right here or from
flat on your back!

Ali throws a punch that doesn't land
because he's separated.

ALI (Cont'd)
What's my name?!?

CLOSE ON ALI
something else is in his eyes.

**INT. THE HOUSTON ASTRODOME - TERRELL -
NIGHT**

hit FOUR TIMES by Ali: WHAM,
WHAM, WHAM, WHAM! In the glaring
lights...

ALI
What's my name, motherfucker?!

And Ali flicks out punches...disorient-
ing Terrell. The BELL.

GIRL IN BANGLED MINISKIRT STARTS 15TH ROUND

WHAM! WHAM! WHAM! Ali hits him
five times...Terrell ties him up. Ali
throws him off, slips two jabs and
snaps his left into Terrell's face.

ALI (Cont'd)
What's my name?

Ali, at the apex of his athletic skills,
fires six- or eight-punch combinations
and then changes direction. Ali shoots
jabs and hooks going backwards;
every move and set of combinations is
a dance. Ali's never been as light on
his feet, as fast, as complex as in this
fight. Like any moment of greatness,
we want it to last forever...Then, Ali
throws a 17-punch combination.

ALI (Cont'd)
WHAT'S MY NAME?!

...that burns down Terrell. Terrell starts
to fall. Ali moves away. He doesn't
want it to end. Sportswriters don't like
it. Half the fans don't like it. Ali defies
both their sensibilities and their politics.

TERRELL'S
face is battered. Ali SLAMS in SHOTS.

ALI (Cont'd)
(shouted)
My name?! WHAT'S MY NAME?!

The BELL ends the savage pounding.
Ali in the middle of the ring, glorying
in opposition and triumph.

INT. HOUSTON COURTROOM - ALI - DAY

with Eskridge and his other attorneys.
The courtroom's packed. In the back
we spot Joe Smiley, anonymous in the
crowd.

ALI
(to Judge)
If the court would give me my sentence right now instead of waiting and stalling.

JUDGE INGRAHAM
(obliges)
My pleasure. The jury has found you guilty of refusing induction into the United States armed forces. I sentence you to the maximum sentence allowable... five years' imprisonment and a fine of ten thousand dollars.
(pause)
Fast enough? Your attorney will lodge an appeal. While you're out on bond, I order your passport be surrendered. I'll not have you benefitting yourself by fighting abroad...

INT. HOUSTON COURT, FOYER – ALI – DAY

on his way out of the building. Media is held at the other end.

CLOSER – ALI

looks dazed, not sure how to act on the way out of court. Oddly, he shakes hands with each of a half a dozen white Houston Bailiffs. It's as if, benumbed by the verdict, he seeks human contact. The only contact avail-able, ironically, is with the officers of the court that just convicted him.

EXT. 79TH STREET, CHICAGO, 1968 – ALI – DUSK

Time has passed. It's winter. Snow's on the ground. He's in a car coat and a hat with a hooded sweatshirt underneath. Street lights are on. Traffic's slight. He walks through the white-ness as new snow falls.

ECU: ALI

under the hat brim, his gaze is internal, as it was in the opening in Miami.

BURNED-OUT STOREFRONT

with icicles from Fire Dept. water. His work boots step deep in the new falling snow...vanishing in the WHITE-OUT...

INT. N.O.I. BAKERY, CHICAGO – WHITE SILK SCARF – DAY (FLASHBACK)

in Ali's hands. He leans across a white showcase of bakery goods. It's cold outside; warm inside. It smells of bread and coffee. BELINDA BOYD reacts.

ALI
Watch now...

He makes a fist, balls the scarf up, and puts it in the hollow of his fist.

ALI (Cont'd)
(offering)
Blow on it...

She blows on it. She's not quite eight-een, six feet tall; there's a supremely confident expressiveness about her. Her gestures are large. He opens his hand. The scarf is gone. She instinc-tively looks over at his other hand. Nothing's there. His eyes go wide in mock fright at the mysterious.

ALI (Cont'd)
This spooky! Don't get scared...

She laughs. How'd he do it? He makes a fist again, puts his thumb in the hol-low. And slowly pulls the scarf out...

BELINDA
(laughs)
See, you don't need to fight no more...

He gives it to Belinda. She ties it around her neck. Ali looks at her. On a cold and dark afternoon, the win-dows are steamed and the bakery seems a fine refuge.

ALI
So what's fresh, girl?

BELINDA
(smiles)
Everything fresh!

ALI
(smiles)
What's the freshest of the freshest?

BELINDA
(smiles)
Doughnuts just came out...

ALI
(holds up the doughnut)
Feed me those things, I gotta come back as a wrassler.
(a ring announcer)
645 pounds. I'd still be pretty... but I be fat pretty...

BELINDA
You don't remember when you met me once before...long ago...

ALI
(joking)
I remember something... Wha's your name?

She slaps his arm.

BELINDA
You know my name! You came to my school, right before you win the title. Interviewed you for the school paper. I was eleven.

ALI
You had a long braid...

BELINDA
Yeah! You called me little Indian girl, then.

ALI
That was you?

BELINDA
I loved you then, like all those kids. I never stopped. I still do.

INT. NATION OF ISLAM ASSEMBLY – ALI + BELINDA – DAY (FLASHBACK)

ELIJAH MUHAMMAD'S VOICE (OVER)
(finishes)

The African-American Albert Speer— regimented seating breaks up. Ali's wearing a black suit, a white shirt and white tie. As he drifts through the crowd, approaching him is Belinda in a white caftan and a white satin turban with gold earrings. It feels like they are an official couple, eugenically chosen mates.

ECU: THEIR HANDS

join.

MACRO CU: SHOULDERS

touch. She turns and leans back slightly against him...Their thighs touch.

EXT. 79TH STREET, CHICAGO – DUSK INTO NIGHT

We walk past the bakery. It's closed. Ali crosses the grey guttered street and exits into...

INT. ALI'S SINCLAIR STATION, BACK OFFICE – ALI – NIGHT

enters. CTA bus passes. Eskridge is there, waiting for him. Ali takes a coffee in a paper cup and grabs a Danish.

ALI
You see the Ellis–Quarry fight?

CHAUNCEY ESKRIDGE
Yes...We'll be in front of the U.S. Court of Appeals next month. We'll lose. Then we appeal to the Supreme Court.

ALI
Ellis the champ? Man. I beatin' on him since we was sixteen. They give Ellis to Joe Frazier? Frazier'll kill him. Then they out of juice. Where's the gate? So they gotta let me fight. I fight Ellis in a phone booth...middle of Times Square...you think that draw a crowd?

CHAUNCEY ESKRIDGE
Draw a crowd or not draw a crowd, Muhammad, is NOT going to make a difference with your boxing licenses. They don't want you to fight.
(so much for speculation)
ACLU's handling your case against the New York Boxing Commission. They discovered New York's got actual ex-murderers and ex-rapists currently licensed to fight. But revoked yours...?

ALI
Tijuana?

CHAUNCEY ESKRIDGE
No. State Department refused permission for the one-hour visa. No fight in Tijuana. Look...

ALI
Can't fight here. Can't fight outside the country...

CHAUNCEY ESKRIDGE
I know people in the restaurant business...want to start up a chain. Muhammad Ali's "Champ

Burger"..."Muhammad Malts," "Fist Full of Fries" ...all of that.

They start out towards the gas pumps.

ALI
Why I want to be in the restaurant business?!

CHAUNCEY ESKRIDGE
'Cause you need the money.

ALI
How much all this gonna cost?

CHAUNCEY ESKRIDGE
Too much. They do that to you, too, you know.

They seek to destroy every facet of Ali's life. Ali knows that. As they pass the pumps. Some customers recognize him.

CHAUNCEY ESKRIDGE (Cont'd)
Where you goin'?

ALI
(to customers)
Look out!

CUSTOMER
Hey, champ!

And Ali pretends to start sparring. The working men laugh. One is brave enough to raise his hands, too. Ali smiles and trades a couple of phantom slaps. It breaks off. He made their day. He shakes each of their hands. His spirit's raised, he walks off. Chauncey watches this ritual...

INT. CHICAGO APARTMENT, ALI + BELINDA'S BEDROOM – NIGHT

hands and skin and faces against white in bed. So close we are intimately inside the moment...

ALI
Not then...

BELINDA
First time? 1961...Sister Khalilah introduced you at assembly. You said you would be heavyweight champion of the world by the time you were twenty-one!

ALI
I always tell the truth...

BELINDA
I was eleven. I interviewed you for the student paper. You called me "little Indian girl," 'cause I wore my hair real long, in a

braid...I told you..."Man, you scribble! You can't even write! You ought to go back to school until you do it better..."

Laughing, he starts poking her in the ribs, and she turns onto him. She's six feet tall; he's six-three. He grabs her wrist. She wrestles him down on the large bed until there's a NOISE, and Belinda separates from Ali and approaches a smaller bedroom to replace the bottle their daughter, MARYUM, threw out of her crib. As she exits, MOVE IN on the crib in streetlight and we HEAR Jimi Hendrix's bottleneck instrumental part of "All Along the Watchtower." It makes us feel the child in the crib is threatened, and that takes us INTO...

INT. COLLEGE HALL - ALI

in a black leather jacket with a white shirt and skinny tie, speaking to an audience of college students, white and black, some Asian and Latino.

JIMI HENDRIX
(from "All Along the Watchtower")
"There must be some kind of
way outta here,
said the joker to the thief..."

Bingham waits in the wings. Applause. Ali joins Howard and a small group watching a portable TV...

TV: "DAYS OF RAGE"

occurring on Chicago's North Clark Street. Off-screen we HEAR police sirens. On TV, Weathermen attack lines of Chicago police! The cops fall back.

JIMI HENDRIX (Cont'd)
"There's too much confusion,
I can't get no relief.
Business men, they drink my wine,
plowmen dig my earth,
None of them along the line,
know what any of it is worth."

INT. CHICAGO GYM - ALI - NIGHT

trains in grey sweats to Hendrix. He finishes 60 sit-ups hanging off a table. He sweats profusely. He has no trainers. Bingham holds his legs. Ali seems heavier.

The gym is grimy, filled with other boxers, a forest of heavy bags, Ali's one among other guys working out.

ALI'S FACE

grimacing through another set, trying to stay in shape, trying to retain skills going dormant.

JIMI HENDRIX
"No reason to get excited,
the thief, he kindly spoke.
There are many here among us,
who feel that life is but a joke."

Then, he's slow on the heavy bag. Sparring alone in the ring...Everyone ignores him.

INT. ALI'S GAS STATION - ALI'S TV: NEWS - DAY

REVEAL Ali + Bingham watching the 1968 Olympics. NOW, Tommy Smith and John Carlos bow their heads and raise fists in black power defiance, instead of acknowledging the national anthem.

JIMI HENDRIX
"But you and I, we've been
through that,
and this is not our fate.
So let us not talk falsely now,
the hour it's getting late..."

And the coverage cuts to George Foreman with a small American flag in his hand. Then, it flashes back to Ali in the ring with Sonny Liston at his feet. And Ali coming out of the Illinois Boxing Commission, angry. Dead Black Panthers, Fred Hampton and Matt Clark murdered by police in Chicago. And Malcolm X and Ali together. The meaning of it is clear: MUHAMMAD ALI IS THE WARRIOR SAINT IN THE REVOLT OF THE BLACK ATHLETE IN AMERICA. On Ali watching, as a phone rings...

JIMI HENDRIX (Cont'd)
"All along the watchtower,
princes kept the view,
while all the women came and went,
barefoot servants, too."

EXT. MEMPHIS MOTEL - CHAUNCEY ESKRIDGE - DAY

speaks to Ali on a pay phone on ground level.

CHAUNCEY ESKRIDGE
...struck out at the appellate level in New Orleans. So we're heading back to the Supreme Court...

INTERCUT WITH:

INT. ALI'S GAS STATION - ALI - DAY

ALI
Thought we already got turned down there.

EXT. MEMPHIS MOTEL - CHAUNCEY ESKRIDGE

CHAUNCEY ESKRIDGE
I'm petitioning on a conscientious objection basis. Religious belief. We'll petition that your sincere religious belief prohibits you from shooting people. I believe they'll hear that...

A fast car drives by, distracting Ali momentarily. Then, Ali focuses 100% on...

ALI
Where the money come from, Chauncey? Herbert tell me I'm runnin' on empty. Put aside "how do that happen"? Licenses all revoked. No passport. I can't fight here. Can't fight abroad.
(beat)
And what happen if I lose the Supreme Court?

CHAUNCEY ESKRIDGE
It's all over. You go to jail for five years.

There's no response from Ali. Ali hangs up, looks the other way, lost in thought.

EXT. MEMPHIS MOTEL ROOM - CHAUNCEY ESKRIDGE - DAY

hangs up the phone. Looks up. Starts to dial another number. A sound CRACKS OPEN THE NIGHT...

Chauncey runs up the stairs to the second-floor balcony to join...

EXT. MEMPHIS MOTEL, BALCONY - JESSE JACKSON - DAY

cradling Martin Luther King, Jr. in his arms. People SCREAM. King involuntarily spasms. Under King, dark blood pools like crude oil. Eskridge, ANDREW YOUNG and JULIAN BOND point into the Memphis afternoon.

EXT. ALI'S APARTMENT BUILDING, ROOFTOP (CHICAGO) - CITY AT NIGHT

as if they were pointing at a burning fire, sirens, blue police flashers, an isolated gunshot. And REVEAL Ali on a rooftop, in sweatpants, sweatshirt, SHADOWBOXING while...

JIMI HENDRIX
"Outside in the cold distance,
a wild cat did growl,
two riders were approaching,
and the wind began to HOWL!"

He leaves off to look into the distance. The agility, what he was with Terrell, isn't there. He exhales in time with punches HUH, HUH, HUH...Ali's struggling to hold onto diminishing sharp-

ness. Police lights. Looting? He con-templates the fabric of the city ripping itself apart while...

INT. JEFFREY STREET HOUSE, LIVING ROOM – FRAZIER RIPS APART ELLIS – NIGHT

on ABC. REVEAL Ali with Maryum in his arms watches the fight...an activi-ty from which Ali, the resident genius on the planet, is excluded.

> **BINGHAM**
> Ellis doesn't belong in there.

> **ALI**
> (curt)
> Man give him a shot, he took the shot.

> **BINGHAM**
> I saw Bundini in New York.

> **ALI**
> How's he?

> **BINGHAM**
> ...bad shape. You better get your belt b-b-back...

Belinda brings coffee to Bingham...

> **BELINDA** (O.S.)
> She's got to be done with that bottle.

> **BINGHAM**
> You call your parents, Ali?

> **BELINDA**
> No, he didn't. I told them about the one on the way...myself.
> (moves to the kitchen)

> **BINGHAM**
> You p-p-p-promised you'd call them.

> **ALI**
> I'll call 'em, I'll call 'em...
> (re: the baby)
> May-may! It go in one end and come out the other.

> **BELINDA**
> You wanna try changing her, for the experience?

> **ALI**
> You so much better at it, mama.

Belinda takes Maryum. FRAZIER holds his arms up in victory, a for-mality of applause from the half-empty Garden.

> **ALI** (Cont'd)
> (to Maryum)
> Maaan...Joe Frazier can't talk, can't up the gate, can't fill the arena. They gotta let me fight.

> **BELINDA**
> That happen, you promise me you put some new people around you.

Ali crosses to kitchen phone.

> **ALI**
> I need Angelo, Rudy, Ferdie —

> **BINGHAM**
> Ali, she's talking about "Brother" Herbert.

Ali stops. Between him and Belinda, this is important: her solidarity is with her husband, not with the NOI.

> **BELINDA**
> Where are they when we need them? You got Gene Kilroy dropping off groceries like charity. Borrowin' money from my folks. So...?

As Ali contemplates what she's said, we HEAR...

> **HOWARD COSELL** (V.O.)
> What are your feelings about up-and-coming Ken Norton?

INT. FRAZIER LOCKER ROOM (POST FIGHT) – COSELL + FRAZIER – NIGHT

FRAZIER
(still sweating)
Norton's big and strong, but...

Someone's talking into Howard's period headset.

HOWARD COSELL
(interrupting)
Hold on one second...we have a caller. Go ahead.

ALI (V.O.)
(into phone)
Cosell? This Muhammad Ali.

A still photo of Ali in an iris appears superimposed on monitors.

ALI (Cont'd)
Go to Georgia or Alabama or Sweden. Everybody know I'm the champ. The crown is a lie. I know it's a lie. Joe Frazier know it's a lie. It time for everybody to stop lying and tell the truth.

HOWARD COSELL
Let's tell it like it is. With your court and boxing problems, Muhammad, can you get a fight promoted?

ALI
I ain't interested in the paycheck, I'd fight Joe Frazier for free in a phone booth in Times Square, if I wasn't broke. I still will.

HOWARD COSELL
Did you say you were broke? How can you be broke?

Ali hesitates.

INT. ELIJAH MUHAMMAD'S HOUSE – KITCHEN – NIGHT

Elijah Muhammad reacts to the interview on television. There's a formality to Elijah Muhammad, even at his kitchen table.

HOWARD COSELL
You've made more money than all previous heavyweight champions combined. What about your management? Surely they have provided for you...

ALI
I'm saying it's time for everybody to quit lying! Muhammad Ali is the champ! I have to, I'll get the fight on myself.
(beat)
And if they offer me money, I ain't gonna turn it down.

CROSSCUT: Elijah turns to an aide.

ELIJAH MUHAMMAD
Get me my son, Herbert, on the telephone!

INT. RUNDOWN CHICAGO GYM – ALI – DAY

training. There is NO entourage with him. Ali hits the heavy bag. He doubles up the left jab on the taped-together heavy bag. Sweat stains his sweats.

EXT. U.S. STEEL – ALI – DAY

runs through tall reeds in the abandoned industrial landscape, ending at the lakefront and the cold, open sky and water. He's breathing hard, struggling against time to hold onto shape and prowess. He seems vulnerable against the open sky and water.

INT. TEMPLE #2 – NIGHT

Elijah Muhammad is at the lectern ringed by Fruit of Islam Guards. HERBERT is behind him.

ELIJAH MUHAMMAD
Mr. Muhammad Ali desires to do that which the Holy Qur'an teaches him against. I am, therefore, suspending Mr. Ali from the practice of Islam. He may no longer appear in temple, pray or teach, or have any conversation with any Muslim whatsoever. Furthermore...he may no longer use the name of Muhammad Ali. Henceforward, he will revert to his old slave name, Cassius Clay.

INT. JEFFREY ST. HOUSE, KITCHEN – ALI – DAY

sits at the table. A deep vacancy is beginning to be there we've never seen before. May-may makes a mess.

BELINDA
Muhammad...?

ALI
You can't call me that no more.

BELINDA
Hell I can't. I'm defying them by talking to you. And being with you.

MOVE CLOSER and CLOSER into Ali's eyes. He's oblivious. Belinda's pregnant again. She says something to him. Ali can't hear. She says it again, louder. Ali doesn't look at her. OVER ALI onto the Formica table with Log Cabin syrup and powdered sugar and ceramic salt and pepper shakers SEEN in his ECU, disconnected, depressed, withdrawn...

INT. FLOPHOUSE, FOYER – ALI + BINGHAM – DAY

entering, concerned and urgent...

ALI
Whyn't you call an ambulance or a doctor?

LANDLADY
(following behind)
Wouldn't let me. Said he knew you...and to call you, Mr. Ali...He's not been out for three days...

Ali's up the stairs, down the corridor and takes the key from the lady and opens the door. It's a dump. Rotting food, something burned on the stove. On the floor, wrapped in a threadbare bedspread, half in and out of the bathroom, which is foul, is Bundini, sleeping off a drunk.

BINGHAM
Bundini!

BUNDINI
(opens his eyes; half sits)
Watchu' doin' here? Gimme that short dog!

Ali—his concern crashes. He detests the type Bundini resembles. He throws a half-empty half-pint of Old Taylor against the wall. It splatters...

ALI
What's wrong with you, man?!

BUNDINI
Nothin' wrong with me!

Ali goes to the curtains and pulls them back. Bundini, blinded...

BUNDINI (Cont'd)
What that?!!!

BINGHAM
A mystery...d-d-d-daylight...

BUNDINI
(shielding his eyes)
Leave me alone!

ALI
I leave you alone. You called me!

BUNDINI
That were a week ago...

Ali grabs Bundini's arm and twists it and pushes his sleeve up. Bundini tries to pull his arm away. Ali is way stronger. Track marks up and down Bundini's arm. Ali slaps Bundini on the side of the head. SMACK! He slaps him again. SMACK!

ALI
What you shame yourself like this for, maaan...?! Why you shame yourself?!

Bundini flails back with his arms. Ali leans in and SMACKS him again.

BUNDINI
Lemme alone!
(shouts)
I'm flyin'! The Sky Chief talk through me. I know the word!

ALI
You know "low." You so low, the curb look like up!

BUNDINI
(demonstrates)
Yeah? The king gotta go home to his throne! From the root to the fruit...!

ALI
Those rhymes is old. Forget 'em.

BUNDINI
(demonstrates more)
God don't care about you! Don't care about me! In all of everything, we mean nothin'. He don't know us. We be. And that's the onliest thing he did. And that's good 'cause that's why we free. But free ain't easy. Free is real. And realness is a motherfucker...
(low; almost spooky)
It eats raw meat.
(beat)
It walk in its own shoes.
(beat)
It does not waver...
(pause)
Yeah...

There's a pause in the room. Bundini crashes. He starts crying, unabashedly...

BUNDINI (Cont'd)
I sold your belt for five hundred dollars to a barber on Lenox Avenue. That's how low I did you. I'm filled with weakness and got a crazy mind. That belt say you the Heavyweight Champion of the World. Five hundred dollars and I put it into my arm. That's what I called to tell you...

Ali leans back against the wall...the last vestige, gone.

BUNDINI (Cont'd)
...heard 'bout the Nation, all that court stuff.

ALI
(absent)
Yeah.

BUNDINI
Forgive me, Muhammad. Take me back...

ALI
No. There's no "back" to take you to...

Ali gets up—Bundini has been taken from him, too—and leaves.

INT. "EL" - ECU FRONTAL: ALI - NIGHT

and beyond the side of Ali's face, elevated through the slums and decrepit tenements of the south side of Chicago...the mean alleys and decaying back porches. Men gathered around 50-gallon steel drums, burning wood for warmth. Everything is corrupted or has left him.

FRONTAL: ALI

staring into nowhere.

REVERSE: PAST ALI

The city recedes. Vectors, in perspective, carry structures, buildings away. The sky is grey, going to blue. The city flees and SUDDENLY disappears as we race into the dark tunnel of subway. Ali's lost in the depths of attempting a calculation. He can't do that for which he has a genius beyond other men...

ALI
(to himself)
...you can't do what you do best in the world. And how you feed your family? From prison? Who take care of your kids? And is Allah, is God with me?

And he's been exiled from the belief system that explained the universe to him. SUDDENLY LIGHTS slash across his face in the white-tile North Avenue station. BEYOND, ghostlike working men and two heavyset women enter. Ali turns aside to prevent being recognized. It's the first time he's ever avoided the public. The train lurches forward...

OVER ALI: WHITE LIGHT

screams away from us. Red reflects off the rails past Ali's face as we descend deeper into the tunnels.

EXT. NEAR BROADCAST TRUCK - COSELL - NIGHT

steps out of the truck. There is a small crowd of people who turn as ALI pulls

up in a convertible. He's solemn for a moment. Then he's out of the car...

ALI (O.S.)
A thousand dollars to the man who brings me Howard Cosell's toupee! Dead or alive!

Reveal Ali next to his car.

HOWARD COSELL
(loud)
Don't bother me. I'm a world-famous broadcaster and you're an ex-champion with diminished skills. I can't be seen with you, it would be calamitous to my reputation.

EXT. NEAR BROADCAST TRUCK - ALI + COSELL - LATER

alone in the convertible parked in a distant corner of the lot.

ALI
Put me on, Howard.

HOWARD COSELL
Muhammad, I'd do anything for you. But I got bosses who only give a damn about Nielsen ratings.

ALI
I guarantee...it will be a historical and a momentous night!

INT. ABC-TV STUDIO

Ali being interviewed by Howard Cosell in the "Wide World of Sports" set. We've entered mid-scene...

ALI
...what Heavyweight Champion of the World? I'm not the champ. I am retired, finished, out of the game. And I ain't gonna let myself grieve and suffer none. But I know I will not fight again...

HOWARD COSELL
I thought you were resolute in your resolve to regain your crown...

ALI
If tomorrow they say: "We want you to fight Joe Frazier. Madison Square Garden. Millions and millionses of dollars. Here's your license back." I will tell them: "I am sorry, but I am done."

HOWARD COSELL
What about Frazier?

ALI

You'll have to wonder...what me
and Smokin' Joe would have
looked like.

HOWARD COSELL

You surprise me, Muhammad...

ALI

Howard, you losing your hearing
along with your hair? Don't put
questions to it!
(beat)
I am through fighting. 'Cause I
got a bigger and more important
match comin' up. The U.S. government. A heavier contender.

HOWARD COSELL

Do you think you're going
to jail?

ALI

I don't know, but it's going to be
a shocking and terrible fight. In
fact, they might wish they let
me stay in boxing.

HOWARD COSELL

Joe Frazier told me on this show
he would knock you out.

ALI

There you go, agitatin'.
(beat)
You ask Smokin' Joe what he
been smokin'?! Joe Frazier
even dream he can whup me?
He better wake up and apologize...
(pause)
But, if I WAS to jump in the
ring with Joe, here's what
you might see...
(recites)
Ali comes out to meet Frazier,
    but Frazier starts to retreat;
If Frazier goes back an inch farther,
    he'll wind up in a ringside seat;
Ali swings with a left, Ali swings
    with a right.
Frazier keeps backin', but there's
    not enough room.
It a matter of time before Ali
    lowers the boom;
Now Ali lands with a right, what
    a beautiful swing,
But the punch lifts Frazier clean
    out of the ring.
Frazier's still risin', but the
    referee wears a frown,
'Cause he can't start countin' 'til
    Frazier come down.
And Frazier's disappeared from
    view. And the crowd is getting
    frantic.
Then our radar stations pick
    him up. He's somewhere over
    the Atlantic.

Who would have thought when
    they came to this fight,
That they would witness the
    launching of a black satellite?

There's laughter off-camera in the studio and a wry smile on Cosell's face.

ALI (Cont'd)

But don't wait for that fight.
'Cause it ain't never gonna
happen. You only can wonder
and imagine...

The phones in the master control
booth are ringing off the hook...the
public's reaction to Ali's Bre'r Rabbit
routine. Ali used his ability to command presence in media to promote
the only fight the public wants to
see...

EXT. CLAY HOUSE – CASSIUS, SR. – DAY

ALI (V.O.)

You want me to buy you a drink?

Ali's dad sits on a crate, painting the
door of a delivery truck. He looks
up...Ali is there. Emotion wells up in
both men. The younger "rebelistic"
son, seeing his father, who is so like
him. The older hep-cat who got cheat-
ed by life of his potential and promise.
In this case, his boy, his boy's name,
pride and reflected glory...

CASSIUS CLAY, SR.

I don't drink no more.
(squints at him)
You wanna fight?

ALI

I don't wanna fight no more.
Not with you...

As they embrace, Odessa comes out,
watches them.

EXT. BROAD STREET – PHILADELPHIA – DAY

Ali stands on the street corner,
shades, incognito. A gold Cadillac pulls
up: JOE FRAZIER. He is wearing a
lemon yellow cowboy outfit, Stetson
hat, striped pants. Ali looks at him in
disbelief.

ALI

Who dress you, Joe? You look
like Dale Evans.

FRAZIER

Shut up. Get in.

Ali gets in, Frazier takes off. He sits
sideways on the seat, steers with one
finger, flicks on the radio: Isaac Hayes.

FRAZIER (Cont'd)

What the hell you in Philly for?
Philly my town.

ALI

To be closer to you, honey.

FRAZIER

Fuck you.

ALI

There be two undefeated heavyweight champions! And they
ain't fighting!

FRAZIER

I wanna fight you! Said it a
hundred times. The Man won't
let you fight no more. What
you complainin' to me for?

ALI

'Cause you gotta get behind this
and we gotta do this.

Frazier screeches to a stop in the middle of Columbia Avenue.

FRAZIER

We..."gotta" do nothin'!!!

ALI

You wanna get this on, Joe?
You and me? Or not?!

FRAZIER

What about your license?

ALI

I can fight in Atlanta.

FRAZIER

How's that? What about the
Boxing Commission?

ALI

Georgia ain't got no state boxing
commission. And Atlanta got a
black city council; a liberal
Jewish mayor, Sam something. It
all set. I do a prelim in Atlanta
with Jerry Quarry. But we got to
get the steamroller movin' now.

FRAZIER

What I got to do?

ALI

You announce if I beat Quarry
you give me the title shot.
(puts it to him)
So what you say...maaan?

Frazier stops in front of his renovated
duplex in the North Philadelphia ghetto.

FRAZIER

My daddy was a sharecropper.

I worked in a slaughterhouse...
right on that corner. I came
up from nothing.
(raises fist)
What I got, I got with this. And I
already got the title. So I got nothing to win and everything to lose.

ALI

But you know you ain't the
champ yet.

FRAZIER

(looks at him)
Yeah..."yet."
(beat)
All right. You beat Quarry, I'll
get inna ring and fuck you up...

They drive off. After a moment,
Frazier looks sideways at him.

FRAZIER (Cont'd)

(quieter)
You need any money or
anything to tide you by...?

ALI

(turns away)
I'm fine. Thanks.

And Ali rests a hand on Frazier's
shoulder, and they drive off like that.

INT. FIFTH STREET GYM – ALI + LARRY
HOLMES – DAY

sparring. Ali's sweating more than we
have seen him sweat before. It's pour-
ing off him. It stains wet his grey
sweatsuit. INTO HIS EYES, through the
headgear...

WIDER

Bingham takes pictures. Sarria, Rudy
and the media in force are there for
the start of Ali's comeback.

FROM BEHIND ALI'S HEAD GEAR

Ali spots...a figure step through the
door. It's Bundini. Ali, seeing everything all the time, reacts not at all,
turns his back. Bundini is thin, drawn,
stooped, but clear-eyed. Everyone
turns. It takes tremendous courage for
Bundini to walk to the ring, expecting
another rejection.

ANGELO DUNDEE

TIME!!

Ali goes to Angelo in his corner.

ANGELO DUNDEE (Cont'd)

Weight's comin' down. 222.

Ali first acknowledges Bundini. Ali moves
down the rope, scowls down at him.

ALI

What you want?

BUNDINI

Take me back, boss.

ALI

You want me to take you back?

BUNDINI

I'm clean.
(beat)
And you a resurrection. This is
God's act. Anybody love poor
people and little people and
fucked-up people gotta be a
prophet. And the prophet is
going home. You the sun.
Let me live in the light.
(pause)
Take me with, boss.
(beat)
...I'll do anything.

Ali considers this man: all jive and
bullshit and also his shaman and resident poet.

ALI

(quietly)
You can't hit what you can't see.

Bundini slowly comes alive, then:

BUNDINI

(quietly)
Float like a butterfly, sting
like a bee.

They look at each other.

ALI/BUNDINI

(quietly)
Rumble, young man, rumble!

INT. CITY AUDITORIUM, ATLANTA – ALI +
QUARRY – NIGHT

We've entered mid-fight in the second
round. We're VERY CLOSE. Quarry has
Ali against the ropes. Ali pushes him
off. Quarry comes in again. Ali dances,
feints and catches Quarry over his
right eye with a jab thrown while
going backwards!

QUARRY

shakes it off. Reorganizes. Throws two
jabs, a right to the body and tries to
follow it up with a left hook. Ali ties
him up. The ref separates them.
Quarry comes in again. Ali throws a
left cross over Quarry's right, which
Ali leaned away from, and adds two
rapid, glancing jabs to the same spot.
And Ali OPENS A CUT. The BELL
sounds, ending Round Two.

CROWD

goes nuts, that part that's pro-Ali:
Atlanta's black elite and scattered
whites. And the thunderous noise
becomes one sound, one momentum,
cheering their warrior saint, their
defiant champion's return. And their
ROAR becomes THUNDER...a momentum unto its own, driving...

ALI'S CORNER: ALI

can't wait for the bell to ring. He sucks
in a huge breath through his nose and
blows it out. Angelo applies Vaseline.

BUNDINI

You the man! You Superman!
Ain't no kryptonite in this ring
tonight!

The BELL sounds Round Three.

INT. THE RING – OVER ALI

Past him, hearing him, we ARE him.
We think what he thinks; see what he
sees. Quarry's corner worked on the
cut. Ali feints a left and throws a left
cross over Quarry's attempt to block
it. Quarry comes in again. Ali's next
three ripping left jabs almost like
karate shots...all with a sharp snap at
the point of impact...

QUARRY'S EYEBROW

streams blood...Interposing himself
between their arms...

REFEREE

stops the fight. Irish Jerry Quarry
damned by skin that cuts and bleeds.

CROWD

goes nuts! Their champion has returned. ALI throws his arms in the
air. QUARRY'S arguing not to have the
fight stopped. Now he appeals to Ali!

CLOSE: ALI + QUARRY

Ali knows Quarry's anguish. They
embrace. Ali says things to him. And
for that moment they are an island.
Ali and Quarry, their arms inter-
locked, are their own tribe. Two
pugilists, no longer adversarial, a
class unto themselves. Then...

ALI'S

picked up by Angelo. Bundini's run
into the ring. Ali's arrived. He is coming back.

INT. MUHAMMAD'S DRESSING ROOM – ALI –
NIGHT

seated, being examined by Pacheco, his hands still taped. The dressing room's crowded. Belinda enters, embraces her husband. Then Ali hears a familiar voice. He sees Herbert Muhammad, along with the expressionless Joseph 13X and another NOI Man, have entered.

BELINDA
(low)
...you don't need their management...

Ali squeezes her hand...and Herbert quietly comes over. He's nervous.

HERBERT
As-Saalam Alaikum...Brother Muhammad...

ALI
All praise to Allah...
(a beat, and softly...)
...Alaikum Salaam...

And people, feeling the awkwardness, give them room...moving out of earshot.

HERBERT
(beaming)
The Messenger has lifted the suspension, Muhammad. Congratulations.

ALI
You saying I can be a Muslim again, Herbert?

HERBERT
Yes.

ALI
(cold)
I never stopped. Like I never stopped being champ.

HERBERT
I begged my father to reinstate you.

ALI
When? After I promoted Quarry fight? After I won it?

HERBERT
We can get you Frazier.

ALI
I already got Frazier.

HERBERT
We can get five million dollars for Frazier.

ALI
Are we talking management, talking money or talking religion?

HERBERT
When you...

ALI
(interrupts)
When I got leery and talked up how come I'm broke, then came the suspension. Now, you explain that to me, my brother...?

HERBERT
It's my father...

ALI
(puts a hand on his shoulder)
I love the Nation, Herbert. I love Elijah Muhammad. But it don't own me.

Herbert's convinced he's getting told "no."

ALI *(Cont'd)*
Now, you go on out. And you make the Frazier deal.

The reversal surprises Herbert; angers Belinda.

HERBERT
My brother!

Ali stops him, keeps him distant.

ALI
Yeah...

Herbert and Joseph 13X leave.

BINGHAM
You b-b-becoming a Christian? Forgive and forget?

Belinda stares at him, containing her fury. Ali confronts her look, frankly, then turns to get dressed.

INT. THE DINING HALL – ALI – LATE AFTERNOON

and Belinda, with new twin babies; Maryum; Dundee; Pacheco; Cassius, Sr.; Sarria; and Ali's entourage. They're all around long tables, eating dinner. A large sign over the kitchen counter with "Lana Shabazz' Ten Commandments"...like: #7 "Anyone bringing guestes in for dinner without prior notice will be awarded thwacks on skull with sharpe object." #8 "Please waite, Rome wasn't burnt in a day; it takes a while to burne the roaste." Lana Shabazz answers a phone and brings it to Ali. Ali's got one of the twins, feeding her a bottle and drinking from it, too.

INTERCUT WITH:

INT. ABC WIDE WORLD OF SPORTS SET – COSELL – DAY

HOWARD COSELL
Muhammad, you T.K.O.'ed 'em...

ALI
What are you talking about, Howard? Quarry?

HOWARD COSELL
(reads)
No. "The Supreme Court ruled today in the case of the United States vs. Cassius Clay a.k.a. Muhammad Ali..."
(looks up)
You won an 8–0 unanimous decision. You're free.

INT. THE DINING HALL – ALI – LATE AFTERNOON

takes in the news, thanks Howard and hangs up. It is a shining moment after living under the threat of imprisonment for three-and-a-half years.

ALI
I'm free.

ANGELO DUNDEE
What are you talking about?

ALI
Supreme Court set me free.

BUNDINI
That's 'cause they know the king is gonna go home to his throne. And they know everybody's with you, now. And they wanna be on the RIGHT side!

INT. MADISON SQUARE GARDEN – WIDE – NIGHT

A sea of glitter: the Black royalty of America in their '70's robes. Movie stars 20 rows back. Burt Lancaster is Cosell's color man. Frank Sinatra is working as a still photographer. In the press section are Plimpton types, Schulberg/Mailer types, Lipsyte, Cosell.

MICROPHONE

descends from the overhead lighting grid. The announcer's hand takes it...

ANNOUNCER
Ladies and gentlemen, fifteen rounds of boxing for the heavyweight championship of the world...

ALI looking out the hood of his robe, dancing, shaking it out, loosening up.

ANNOUNCER *(Cont'd)*
...the contender and former heavyweight champion of the world, seeking to regain his title, from Louisville, Kentucky, Muhammad Ali!!!

Catcalls and boos. The other half is a comeback sound. It is a nation divided: pro-war right-wingers, Nixon supporters are for Frazier; the anti-war movement, celebrities, New York liberal establishment, blacks, Puerto Ricans and hippies are for Ali.

ANNOUNCER
And in the opposite corner,
the current heavyweight
champion of the world,
Smokin' Joe Frazier...!

The contentious roar diminishes only slightly for the announcer.

ALI'S EYES

deep in his focused concentration. His attention so arrow like it reminds us of the younger man in the Liston fight...pure purpose.

THE RING

...only SILENCE as the referee's instructions are given in SLO-MOTION. Ali bounces on the canvas. We HEAR his feet shift, turn, dance...and his breathing, expectant. Here comes the return of what was unfairly taken: his heavyweight championship.

DISSOLVE TO:

MID-FIGHT – ALI

looks swollen, out of breath. Something's wrong! Two solid Ali jabs and a right hook connect. But they slow down Frazier not at all. Joe Frazier, short and compact, like a pit bull, bobs and weaves his way inside Ali's longer reach.

ALI'S CORNER – DUNDEE + BUNDINI

shouting instructions. None get through. Ali looks slow. Older.

INT. RING – PROFILE: ALI + FRAZIER

Frazier, off his bobbing and weaving, launches his devastating left hook to Ali's head. Frazier is making the most of what he is: smaller. Ali clinches.

VERY LOW: FRAZIER + ALI

The referee separates them. Both men throw and miss...Ali on the right, Frazier on the left. Ali throws a hard left that catches Frazier but doesn't stop him. Now Frazier connects with a wild left hook into Ali's cheekbone. THE UNTHINKABLE HAPPENS...

OVERHEAD: ALI

is knocked down onto his knee. Ruled a slip, he stands immediately and con-tinues. Ali, backed against the rope again, blocks shots, pushes Frazier into the middle of the ring...

ALI SWINGS FRAZIER

around. But Frazier cranks his left. ALI SEES IT COMING...

ALI
(to himself)
Hook's comin'. Lean back, man!
Move back! WORK LEGS...!

But Ali's legs DON'T work fast enough. Frazier's hook CRASHES into Ali's face. Ali goes rubbery as he backs to the rope. Ali comes out and backs to the rope on the other side, with cartoon rubbery legs. But the mimicry is camouflage. He really is wobbling. The crowd is going wild. We HEAR everything, now.

FRAZIER

is wary. He doesn't trust Ali. He walks across the ring, allowing Ali to recuperate...THE BELL. Ali walks to his corner, drained...

HOWARD COSELL (V.O.)
Ali was out! He was out on his feet. Joe almost had him. Frazier must have thought Ali was playing possum. 'Cause Ali's a clown. Others have come in on Ali when he's playing possum and gotten knocked out.

Ali saved himself with GUILE.

ROUND FIFTEEN:

They clinch. They separate. They both...as if mirror images of each other...crouch, looking for shots. Ali's right is down. Frazier's right is down. As they both rise up off the crouch, Frazier's out of the box first. Ali's right is coming around. Frazier's left hook slams Ali across the jaw. Ali goes down. Half the crowd ROARS for Frazier. Ali gets right up and stands in the corner and takes the mandatory eight-count. The right side of his face is swollen like a balloon. They resume...

OVERHEAD: ANOTHER CLINCH

Ali takes another right, but the ropes hold him up. Another left catches Ali. Frazier's face is a grotesque, swollen mask. He doesn't care.

ALI

is exhausted. Labored breathing. The crowd cheering Frazier.

THEN THE BELL.

Ali drops his arms. He knows he lost. Frazier raises his arms. He knows he won. Half the crowd cheers.

INT. MADISON SQUARE GARDEN, ALI'S DRESSING ROOM – ALI – NIGHT

ANGELO DUNDEE
Hell of a fight, champ...

Not only have we seen Ali lose for the first time, not only do we see him bruised, but when a fighter's beaten, everybody who believes in him is beaten. Angelo's cutting the tape off his hands. Bundini places an ice pack on the back of his neck.

HANGERS-ON
They stole it from you! (etc.)

Bundini's wise enough to say nothing.

ALI
Shut up! I lost.
(louder)
Get outta here...

Rudy heard...

RUDY
Go on! Everybody out!

As they leave, the door reveals packed media outside. Door closes. Now it's only the inner circle.

ANGELO DUNDEE
(to Pacheco)
Ferdie, take a look at this...
(to Ali)
It was still a hell of a fight.

ALI
Where's Belinda?

PACHECO
She fainted...They took her to the aid station. She's okay.

Pacheco looks at Ali's hand. It shakes. Pacheco looks at Ali's eyes and has him follow his finger.

ALI
My hands was in sand, Angie.
My feet in water...

ANGELO DUNDEE
Maybe we shoulda had more time between Blin and this, you know...to get back into...

ALI
Woulda, shoulda, coulda...
(pause)

After three-and-a-half years, this is...from how far back... comeback is.

Ali throws a water bottle. It shatters and splays wet down the wall. There is mature, deep-seated, dead-serious molten anger. Everybody in the room feels it.

INT. CORRIDOR

With Bundini, Bingham, Rudy and Sarria as a wedge, Ali drives through reporters on the way to Belinda. Press mob Ali...

> PRESS
> Were you robbed?

> ALI
> I lost. You lose, you don't shoot yourself. The world goes on.

> ANOTHER REPORTER
> Joe said he didn't think you wanted to fight him again...

> ALI
> *(stops)*
> Oh, how wrong he is.

INT. MADISON SQUARE GARDEN, AID STATION - BELINDA - NIGHT

sees Ali...the beating. She begins crying...

> BELINDA
> My God. They killed you!

Ali moves to her, followed by Bingham and Pacheco. A doctor's approaching with a sedative in a syringe.

> PACHECO
> Get away from her. What is that?

Ali leans over, speaks softly.

> ALI
> I ain't dead, baby! C'mon.

Embracing her, his eyes connect with Dundee. Ali's Supreme Court victory is meaningless. It's drowned by the loss of what the political persecution took from him: his prime, his season that would have been his most brilliant.

INT. SAN DIEGO SPORTS ARENA, ALI VS. NORTON I (2ND ROUND) - TWO FIGHTERS - NIGHT

BLUR in SLO-MO. Focus is beyond, to the crowd.

OVER ALI: OUT-OF-FOCUS KEN NORTON'S RIGHT FIST

starts an arc...or jams towards us.

RIDING NORTON'S FIST - SLO-MO

towards Ali. We PASS crowd, the lighting grid above and SLAM into the side of Ali's jaw, and on the moment of impact...

ECU: X-RAY IMAGE - SLO-MO

of Ali's jaw breaking, shearing, leaving an eighth-inch gap in the bone of the lower mandible...and becomes...

CMS: ALI

taking the shot, covering and assaulting, covering with his left, which he turns into a jab, aggressively going after Norton.

IMAGE TURNS TO WHITE AS...

INT. SAN DIEGO SPORTS ARENA, ALI'S CORNER - WHITE TOWEL

fills the frame. Go behind it as they shield Ali spitting blood into a bucket.

> ALI
> I can move my jaw with my tongue. He got me...

Pacheco looks into his mouth.

> PACHECO
> *(concerned)*
> It's broke. I think...I think your jaw's broke.

Meanwhile, Ali spots...

REFEREE

curious about the activity in Ali's corner, starts over...

PACHECO

nods to Dundee. Dundee starts to reach. Ali snatches Angelo's hand holding the towel. Angelo's about to end the fight...

> ALI
> Ain't stoppin' nothin'...!
> *(glares at them)*
> Nothin' stoppin'...!

A BELL sounds and Ali goes out to fight in an OVERHEAD SHOT.

BURN OUT TO WHITE:

INT. SAN DIEGO SPORTS ARENA, ALI AND HIS CORNERMEN + SECURITY - NIGHT

leave the ring and another defeat, as they move up the aisle towards the locker room...

INT. ALI'S WOODLAWN AVENUE HOUSE (CHICAGO), LIVING ROOM - ALI - DAY

watching television. The place is a huge mansion on Chicago's South Side.

> HERBERT
> Now that Smokin' Joe's run out of tomato cans to beat up, I finally got Yank to commit to a rematch with you in about six months. Frazier said he'd be happy with three mil...
> *(beat)*

WIDEN TO INCLUDE THE LIVING ROOM WITH BINGHAM, ALI'S TWINS—RASHEEDA AND JAMILLAH—MUHAMMAD, JR. AND MARYUM

> HERBERT *(Cont'd)*
> I'll fly to Jamaica and get Yank to sign right after Joe beats this big stiff.
> *(to TV)*

OVER ALI: CONSOLE TV

They watch the Frazier—Foreman fight from Jamaica amid the wonderful chaos generated by kids and their toys, who crawl all over Ali as if he were furniture. Frazier and Foreman are in the center of the ring...We SEE Don King in Frazier's corner.

> ALI
> *(through still-wired-together jaw)*
> Foreman call me one time after he won the Olympics...

Meanwhile, Frazier bobs and weaves, ducks and moves like he did with Ali. Joe throws a left hook, leaning forward with it. Before it lands, Foreman unleashes a hard right that jolts Frazier SIDEWAYS. Frazier throws another hook that misses. Foreman hits him with a combination of right and three lefts...two hooks and an uppercut that LIFTS FRAZIER OFF THE GROUND. Ali leans in to SEE...

> HOWARD COSELL
> *(shouting)*
> DOWN GOES FRAZIER! DOWN GOES FRAZIER!

ON TV: THE RING

Frazier stands. The referee does the mandatory eight-count. Foreman bangs Frazier into the corner and blasts him again. Frazier tries to muscle out of the corner. Foreman lifts and throws him back into the corner. Foreman's power is unreal. Frazier is the man who beat Ali. Now, Frazier feints and slides sideways, and Foreman hits him in the back of the head. Frazier goes down again. It is savage. Here is a new world champion: George Foreman.

> BINGHAM
> *(wry)*
> B-b-be easy gettin' a Frazier

fight now. He ain't the champ of anything except getting knocked down.

INT. MADISON SQUARE GARDEN (ALI–FRAZIER II) – HANDS + ARMS – NIGHT

grabbing. Holding. Ali's got Joe's powerful left tied up this time. A clinch. Separating. A punch. A hook. Clinching. They separate...

OVER JOE:

Ali, having Joe at the right range, hits him. Joe moves in. Ali DRAGS him closer and ties him up. They dance...

THEIR BODIES

Ali does a little shuffle, circles to keep Joe at hitting distance, lands a combination. Joe closes, but Ali won't let him in and ties up Joe. We hear a BELL and that's the end of the fight. Not a bang; a whimper.

REFEREE

holds up Ali's hand and mouths silently words we cannot hear. And as we MOVE CLOSER INTO ALI'S EYES, we see no exaltation. This is a victory, but a hollow one. It's a decision eked out.

INT. NEW YORK COFFEE SHOP – WIDE

The inner circle: Ali, Pacheco, Dundee, Bundini, Bingham.

ALI

So.

ANGELO DUNDEE

So we only eked this one out. And George Foreman makes Frazier look like a sissy.

PACHECO

You see their fight?

HOWARD BINGHAM

You mean the Joe Frazier falling-down lesson?

PACHECO

And Foreman is 24. You are 32 years old. I don't want to see your head get turned into someone's bull's-eye.

ANGELO DUNDEE

...but, you go? We're the corner, same as always. But it ain't gonna be easy.

ALI

(to Angelo)
You think I still got the tools?

ANGELO DUNDEE

You got the tools, Daddy. But they different.

ALI

(thinks; decides: go)
Well, you better sharpen 'em up. 'Cause we goin' to Africa.

BUNDINI

The motherland. From the root to the fruit. We gonna rumble... in the jungle.

ALI

It's time to be heavyweight champion of the world again.

BUNDINI

Yeah, man!

INT. NEW YORK PRESS CONFERENCE – DAY

DON KING

"Rumble in the Jungle!" That's the name I given it.

Ali and Don King hold court with the press. Also there is George Foreman and his trainer, Dick Sadler, and his manager, Nilon.

DON KING (Cont'd)
A historical happening. This event will show that the black man has arrived on the world stage. Muhammad Ali and George Foreman in Kinshasa, Zaire.

PRESS REACTIONS:

where's Zaire?

REPORTERS

Don. Zaire? Why not Antarctica? What's wrong with New York City?

DON KING

Because you miss the significance. I dream, as Martin Luther King once dreamt, that a man could be judged by the content of his mind. This is about black men helping black men, overcoming four hundred years of racial depression to the dawn of a new day of liberation... financial and otherwise.

King getting really evangelistic...

DON KING (Cont'd)
It will raise up the spirit of our inner cities. It will rise up and fill with hope the souls, the unrequited needs of the black proletariat, that is, the discouraged, dispirited, denigrated, denizens of the demimonde, that is called...the ghetto.

Ali's looking at him in amazement.

ALI

Man, you crazy.

Don King laughs. As the press digs King...MOVE ONTO Foreman, and here's what's wrong with all of this...we SEE that Foreman, eight years younger, two inches taller, almost as fast and seemingly twice as strong, is not beatable by Muhammad Ali. Foreman doesn't just hurt you, Foreman can kill you. How is Ali not going to get killed by this man with death in his eyes and indifference on his face? Meanwhile...

DON KING

Ten million dollars. With one stroke of the pen, you split the world's biggest emolumation in the history of sports!

Ali signs a contract; then Foreman. Flashbulbs.

DON KING (Cont'd)
The "Rumble in the Jungle"!

Don King bursts out laughing.

EXT. KINSHASA AIRPORT, TARMAC – ROOF – PAST HEADS – DAY

PUSH THROUGH people and SEE an Air Zaire DC-10 pulling in. A ramp is wheeled up. The plane stops taxiing. Zairian officials in safari suits, paratroopers with white helmets, LT. NSAKALA and hundreds of African, European and American media with cameras and lights approach. The hatch opens. A ROAR emerges from the right and left. We don't see the source.

INT. AIR ZAIRE DC-10'S – ALI

Belinda's behind him. Bingham's there, Bundini, Angelo Dundee, Sarria. As they crowd to the door, we're shooting OVER ALI starting down the ramp. He looks up. We don't see what he sees. We see only the crowd of people at the foot of the ramp, including Don King in a dashiki and the crowd on the tarmac.

FRONTAL: ALI

looking ABOVE the receiving party. The ROAR again. He looks side to side, almost distracted from King and the officials. He waves. Distant CROWD ROAR increases. They're chanting something. We don't understand the words. It contains his name. Now...

PAST ALI: REVEAL A THOUSAND PEOPLE

are beyond the receiving party. They're on the roof of the airport. They're sitting on balconies and fences. They're waving their arms. They're on every possible horizontal surface that can support weight. They're shouting in unison, a syncopated ROAR...his name and something else. Ali moves through the receiving party, as if in a trance, to get through the airport to the other side. Security tries to keep up...

EXT. AIRPORT ENTRANCE + STREET - ALI

emerges and reacts. He's electrified. Dundee, Bingham and a few cops are with him. Everybody else got left behind. REVEAL 10,000 people are OUTSIDE the airport, cheering his arrival. Their cheer is thunder.

ALI
(to Zairian Official; shouts)
What are they saying, man?!!! Why they saying that?

ZAIRIAN OFFICIAL #1
They say, "Ali, boma ye. Ali, boma ye."

ALI
What's that mean?! I don't understand!

ZAIRIAN OFFICIAL #1
It mean...!

ALI
(can't hear)
What?!

ZAIRIAN OFFICIAL #1
(has to shout)
It mean..."Ali, kill him! Ali, kill him!"

Ali moves forward. The Zairian Official and four cops fade back, nervous about being in so large a crowd. The crowd's a tidal wave, carrying Ali forward, supporting, never mobbing him.

MUHAMMAD ALI

is overcome. This is all for him. He is their hero. He defied the world's powerful. They tried and could not destroy him. His defiance made him their champion. And now he has come to contest his rightful title against the numb instrument of the all-powerful. He raises his arm, too, and shouts...

ALI
Ali, boma ye!

Ten thousand voices carry it on the wind and take away Ali's breath.

ALI (Cont'd)
Ali, boma ye!

DON KING, ZAIRIAN OFFICIALS #1 + #2

in the rear realize, as do we, this is NOT MERELY A BOXING MATCH.

CUT TO: INT. AIR ZAIRE DC-10 - NIGHT

A towering man in denims with sequins blocks our view of the door as he walks out onto the ramp. Only now do we see BEYOND HIM a small welcoming party. Native African dancers, a big banner that proclaims, "Welcome, George Foreman," the Zairian paratroopers, media and a few dozen of the curious.

FRONTAL: GEORGE FOREMAN

looks like "Superfly" on steroids. His entourage follows him down the ramp. DICK SADLER, tough and smart, is the Louis Armstrong of trainers. ARCHIE MOORE, crafty and wise, wears a blue shirt and blue pea-cap.

If George Foreman wonders at the paucity of his reception, he doesn't let on.

INT. ALI'S HOUSE, N'SELE - ALI - MORNING

sits in EXTREME CLOSE-UP drinking coffee...lost in thought. He's somewhere else, puzzled, alone in his thoughts. He wears grey sweatpants, a thin-rubber long-sleeved T-shirt under his grey sweatshirt. He's oblivious to the Euro-modern furnishings. Then it's time, and he leaves...

EXT. N'SELE COMPOUND - WIDE: ALI

enters from his bungalow. We SEE we're in a compound. They are white and severely truncated houses linked by sidewalks and too many large street lamps. As Ali starts to jog through this imitation of suburbia with the scale all wrong. It's like a Gulag in reverse for the rich and powerful to be within while keeping the rest of the country out. As Ali passes, REVEAL we are at the bank of the Congo River. As Ali starts his predawn run, across the river the first band of magenta tints the horizon and reflects molten on the water.

TRACKING SHOT: ALI + DUNDEE, SARRIA IN A PICKUP TRUCK - RED DAWN

plus two trainers and the ever-present Zairian POLICEMAN, Lt. Nsakala. The early sun paints the red earth ochre.

ALI
(to himself)
Fast. Six left jabs flash from his chest and shoulder, followed by a right hook and left and right uppercuts.

ALI (Cont'd)
(to himself)
Back up, maaan...
(weaves suddenly; another voice)
...you fast!

Ali slides to the right and throws a left jab and hooks off the jab.

EXT. KINSHASA ROAD - EMPTY ROAD - MORNING LIGHT

Ali ENTERS, running. The road is lined with Mobutu's green billboards in French and English, proclaiming Zaire wonderful. A few kids emerge from behind the signs, coming out from between...and they trail Ali.

KIDS
Ali, boma ye!

ALI
(repeating)
Ali, boma ye George Foreman!

And he throws a couple at an imaginary George Foreman. There are 15 to 16 kids, now.

ALI (Cont'd)
You out, sucker!

Curious, Ali runs behind the green signs from where the kids came.

ALI'S

still jogging. Behind the signs, he becomes a magnetic attraction. People are surprised to see Ali. He's making their day. Euphoric kids parallel him, run with him, follow him...

PAST ALI:

the concrete-and-cinder-block walls on the dusty, bare ground are chromatic. Primary colors. Ethnographically interesting.

ALI SEES interiors. Broken walls. No roof. No plumbing. People come from a ditch with a shower curtain for privacy, surprised to see Ali. Faces indifferent to squalor. This is the ethnographically "interesting" surface of what, in fact, is civic disintegration starting to occur...It is the human concomitant to 13 years of Mobutu kleptocracy.

Le Combat entre FOREMAN et ALI
n'est pas une bataille entre deux ennem
mais un sport entre deux freres.
AN — ALI fight
is not a
een two enem
but spo
two brothe

ALI

looks at the backs of the signs. He and we realize the signs' purpose: to hide the makeshift plastic walls and rooms made from cardboard containers and oil drums from the foreigners traveling the road to Kinshasa. One TEENAGER WITH A WITHERED ARM and a big smile runs up...

TEENAGER
(broken English)
You beat them, Ali!

ALI
Foreman? I kill him!

He mimes knocking out Foreman. Something powerful is affecting Ali. We don't know what it is. Ali slows down...

...throws two lightning jabs and a hook. Ali reaches to the kid's head and pulls a coin. He flips it to another kid and walks on. A SECOND TEENAGER comes out and wants Ali to look at something around the back. He takes Ali's hand...and holds it. Ali complies. The entourage follows...

AROUND CORNER: KIDS' PAINTING ON WALL

It's an imitation fight poster. Childlike caricatures in Basquiat-like brush strokes. Foreman's got crosses for eyes. He's out! Ali is victorious! His fist is raised. His cartoon face shouts his victory...the people's champion. There's more. There's knocked-out white policemen, knocked-out black soldiers, knocked-out landlords, knocked-out South Africa, knocked-out planes and tanks, knocked-out tse-tse flies...everything!

So much, it means "ALL"... all expectation. This childish painting powerfully affects Ali. The kids look at him. It's still. Some kids in the back leap up in the air to see over taller heads what Ali's doing.

ALI

looks at individual faces. A grinning OLDER MAN with a blue transistor radio (we'll see him later). A smiling kid. A girl with no shoes. A teenage kid jumping up and down...all looking at him. Ali makes four pieces of rope appear. He rubs them together...

ALI (Cont'd)
Shazaam!!!

They become one. Everybody goes nuts. As Ali leaves, his eyes go back to the people and the painting...

EXT. KINSHASA ROAD – ECU: ALI'S FACE – MORNING (GREEN SCREEN)

ALI
(to himself)
...even if I die here. If it kill me, no matter what...I gotta win.

Concentration has taken him into the athlete's zone, the state of unified awareness wherein dwells his total self-knowledge. And he knows the transaction: what they give him with their adoration, which he converts to power, is in exchange for what he means to them. And what he means to them is specific: he represents them in defying power and vanquishing what oppresses. He validates the existence of expectation, that struggle is possible...George Foreman, mute and unknowingly, represents disinterested power. Ali doesn't "accept" his obligation; he embraces it. It is his purpose, revealed. And he will never waver from it.

CUT TO:

INT. INTERCONTINENTAL HOTEL, ANTEROOM (KINSHASA) – ALI – DAY

waits, sitting on a table edge in a corridor. Noise of a press conference setting. Howard Cosell crosses through, smoking. Bingham enters and gestures...they're ready. Ali waves off Bingham, stops Cosell...

ALI
Howard! How many you ugly sportswriters in there got me over Foreman? Don't lie.

HOWARD COSELL
(beat)
Some of us...Norman, me...are worried. How you gonna dance against George?? He's sparring with a middleweight, training to cut you off. He gets you against the ropes, he can knock you out with either hand.

ALI
(drops facade)
What's the odds?

HOWARD COSELL
Two-and-a-half-to-one. Against. We're worried you're going to get hurt.

No one thinks Ali will win.

INT. INTERCONTINENTAL HOTEL, MEDIA CONFERENCE ROOM – CLOSE: ALI – DAY

ALI
This'll be the biggest upset since Sonny Liston. I want all of

you to write it down! This fight is no contest!

We've jammed into the middle of Ali in a blast of braggadocio.

ALI (Cont'd)
George Foreman is a big mummy. I've officially named him "The Mummy."

Laughter.

ALI (Cont'd)
George punches are like "Look out, here come the left." Whomp!
(stiff-armed swing)
Here come the right! Whomp! Like a Mummy. But "The Mummy" can't hit what it can't see. I'm fast! Gonna dance. Be all over George. George is gonna feel he surrounded.
(beat)
And I done somethin' new for this fight: I done rassled with an alligator.

Anticipatory laughter. They've had twelve years' experience of Ali's stand-up and know when a new routine's starting...

ALI (Cont'd)
That's right!
(laughter again; Ali almost loses it)
I have rassled with an alligator. I done tussled with a whale. I done handcuffed lightning, thrown thunder in jail. That's bad! Only last week I murdered a rock. Injured a stone. Hospitalized a brick. I'm so mean, I make medicine sick.

Laughter.

HOWARD COSELL
Muhammad, I'm sorry. I have to ask.
(he hesitates; he's sorry, but)
Are you really fast enough, anymore? To beat George Foreman? Many people believe you don't have the same skills, that you are not the man you used to be ten years ago.

There it is. Has doubt, spoken truthfully in the open, closed the mouth of Muhammad Ali? A beat. Then...

ALI
Howard. I didn't want to talk about this, especially in front of everybody. But I talked to your wife! And she told me you're not the man you used to be...two years ago!

The assembled media crack up. Ali's eyes are wide in mock amazement.

CLOSE: COSELL

A bittersweet smile and the eye contact with Ali. Cosell knows...

INT. GYM FLOOR – HEAVY BAG – LATE AFTERNOON

is slammed by a massive fist. It leaves a dent the size of a deflated basketball. The fist is George Foreman's.

DICK SADLER

holds the bag. Foreman throws hooks, one after the other. Each blow rocks Sadler. George is literally punching a hole in the bag. These blows would mash an opponent's liver, break ribs, destroy kidneys. This man can do more than hurt you. This man can kill you.

INT. RING – FOREMAN + SPARRING PARTNER – LATER

Foreman is boxing a middleweight. He is smaller than Foreman and, therefore, faster. And, that's the point. The partner tries to circle, slide, dance away, and Foreman cuts him off and drives him to the ropes where he tags him. He doesn't put a lot behind it. Partner slides...

FOREMAN

darts left and jars him with three left jabs, keeping him on the rope. Foreman's training to defeat Ali's dancing, his "float + sting" tactics.

CLOSE: GEORGE FOREMAN

is young, has unreal power and he can move.

CUT TO:

INT. TRAINING COMPOUND – METAL GRILL DOORS: ALI'S ENTOURAGE

is entering. Lieutenant Nsakala is there, too. They time-share the facility. Foreman's entourage with conga drummers are exiting. Ali and Foreman are never closer than 10 feet apart. Foreman says nothing. Ali starts banging his hands on Foreman's conga and shouts over the percussion at Foreman...

ALI
Salaam Alaikum, brothers!
(raises one arm)
The champ is here!

SIDE ANGLE: THE TWO ENTOURAGES

pass. Comparatively, Foreman looks bigger. He is more dense of bone. He's taller. His chest seems deeper and his shoulders wider.

AND FOREMAN'S EXPRESSION

is casual, unrattled by Ali's antics. He is menacing in his indifference. It means he's ALSO immune to getting psyched out by Ali.

INT. RING – CROWD – LATER

Bundini's in Ali's corner. Ali's sparring partner is Larry Holmes. Ali's hands are at his side. He dances, bicycles, shuffles, dances, dodges, doesn't throw anything, his elbows at his side. Ali is training to DANCE from Foreman. He's fast, but not seemingly suspended in air as he was 10 long years ago against Liston.

INT. N'SELE COMPOUND, ALI'S HOUSE – BELINDA – MORNING

BELINDA
Here's your water.

ALI
Bottled water. Frozen steaks. Brought all this stuff like Africans don't have steaks...

BELINDA
You could pick up parasites...

ALI
They eat it.

BELINDA
You're seeing what you want to see, Muhammad...

ALI
Mobutu eats it...

BELINDA
Mobutu is taking care of Mobutu and stealing all the wealth and sending it to Switzerland...

ALI
(pause)
So? What's that do with any of why we here?

BELINDA
(she doesn't get it)
We're here 'cause Don King got Mobutu to put up ten million dollars. Don King don't give a damn about Africa. He worse than Herbert.

ALI
Here come "Herbert."

BELINDA
Yeah. 'Cause where was he when we was broke and borrowing money? And Bundini and all them that "love you"? Disappeared, is where they were.
(on a roll)
All over you when you got it and drop off you when you don't...

ALI
Money? I do "money-making" whenever I want. Money is easy.

BELINDA
(running on)
And Don King fit right in...that double-breasted hipster is now a dashiki-wearing rip-off.

ALI
Don King delivered the first black-promoted championship fight in Africa!

BELINDA
Don King talks black, lives white and thinks green! Why you defending him and "brother" Herbert?
(against me)

ALI
'Cause clean-cut Muslims parading on the South Side of Chicago don't get this done! I got to put honkeys with connections and bad-ass niggers to it, too.

BELINDA
(not hearing)
And now they got you up against George Foreman. Do they give a damn you could get killed?

ALI
That what this is? Think I gonna lose? Puttin' doubt on me?

BELINDA
(tears flow)
I think: why is my Muslim husband letting himself get strung up on a cross...? It means "tell me."

He won't. Ali picks up his bag and starts out...

BELINDA (Cont'd)
Maryum is sick. Maybe I oughta go back to Chicago and look after her.

ALI
Sure.

BELINDA
I'll be back before the fight.
(sarcastic)
If that's all right, my husband...

He walks out the door.

CUT TO:

EXT. KINSHASA ARENA – 75 ZAIRIAN TRIBAL DANCERS – NIGHT

to percussion. The number.

ALI,

Angelo and Bingham in the empty seating, looking at the ring under the canopy. Behind them is the rehearsal. Meanwhile...

CUT TO:

EXT. ARENA, ENTRANCE – TWO CARS

arrive, including in the first an Interpreter, Zairian Official #2, a Policeman Driver; and in the second car is Don King, Herbert, VERONICA, and another American Woman (silent bit). They're in a hurry...

EXT. ARENA – ALI

is being taught to dance by two dancers. They fail. In the background, workers are raising gigantic Mobutu portraits. The Pointer Sisters begin.

AISLE

Don King and entourage approach.

DON KING
(over the drumming)
Champ! Champ! George had an accident.

ANGELO
(suspicious)
What are you talking about?

Pointer Sisters start "Yes, We Can Can."

DON KING
Got cut. Right above his right eye. His sparring partner's elbow. Split it open, so...

ANGELO DUNDEE
Can he fight?

DON KING
Not for six weeks.

Ali laughs.

DON KING (Cont'd)
This is not a humorous situation, my champion. This postponement could be long, especially if George leaves.

ANGELO DUNDEE
Are you tryin' to pull something, Don? Ali wants his title. And he wants it back in Zaire. George leaves, he ain't comin' back. George don't like it here.

Pointer Sisters' rehearsal cuts...re-organizes.

DON KING
How right you are, my suspicious and short Italian brother. And my fiduciary responsibility to this first all-black promotion is like a garden in the African sun. It must grow! It must bloom! It cannot flower in the gloom and shade of postponement to some dome. Like the Astrodome, the Super-dome, any dome outta Zaire, where it be deprived of light and bled of water. 'Cause what gonna bleed... is money. A hemorrhage of cash.
(sees it all)
...blood on the floor. Double hotel costs. Double travel costs. Airplanes. Food and beverage...

ANGELO DUNDEE
(rhetorical)
What do you expect us to do, Don?

DON KING
(moves close to Ali)
Muhammad. Find a way to get George to stay. Be Moses in reverse: do NOT let my people go! Stay the fuck right here, in Egypt, if you'll pardon my Swahili.

BINGHAM
L-l-l-lingala.

DON KING
What?

BINGHAM
Lingala. They s-s-s-speak Lingala.

DON KING
Who cares?

Pointer Sisters probably end here. After a beat, percussion starts up. Dancers drift in.

ANGELO DUNDEE
(pissed, dissed big)
If George goes? You forfeit five million. You crawl back to Cincinnati. You ain't promotin' a charity raffle...

We see Herbert watching all of this closely...particularly the challenge to Ali/Dundee.

DON KING
(irrepressible)
If George goes? George goes, my

champion, I will get you Joe Frazier. Ali–Frazier III...the fight everybody want to see.

INT. PRESS CONFERENCE

ALI
(interrupts)
Truth is...George knocked hisself out.

Don King laughs, nervously. Ali is daring George to stay.

ALI (Cont'd)
That's right. He did three rounds. Knew he was gonna lose to Muhammad Ali and knocked hisself out. And I predict that whenever the fight is set, he might not show up!

DON KING
(double entendre)
You bad!

ALI
I'm a bad man!

DON KING
Ain't no doubt about it.

ALI
And you tell the same thing to George.

Media laugh, Don King goes along, Ali continues...

ALI (Cont'd)
(to King)
I been watchin' you! I heard you. I know he's your man. I know you got him picked. But the man's in trouble. The whole world was gonna know. But, now, he ain't gonna show. That's why he knocked hisself out when he was training.

DON KING
(laughs to dismiss Ali)
We will reschedule the fight, and to ensure George is ready, we are thinking of postponing from September 24th to October 30th.

REPORTER
What about the concert, Don?

DON KING
That would go off as planned on September 22nd and 23rd.

ALI
(skeptical)
Uh-huh. I want all helicopters guarded! Private boats. Private jets. I want the airport—I'm

161

serious—I want President Mobutu and all his paratroopers. I want all of you "Zaireans" to be on guard! Watch all strange boats tryin' to slip away! They might be takin' him out.

ANGELO DUNDEE
The bus station.

It's Ali kidding on the square. A serious point delivered not seriously to be taken seriously.

ALI
Yeah. Watch the bus station. Watch everything! Elephant caravans. He might sneak out by elephant.

BUNDINI thinks of a line and whispers it to Don. Don leans past Dundee to pass it on to Ali.

ANGELO DUNDEE
What you say?

DON KING
I ain't talkin' to you!

ALI
(to King)
Hey!!!

His eyes flash. He leans forward and puts a finger in Don King's face.

ALI *(Cont'd)*
Don't talk to Angelo like that! Don't you talk to him like that ever again!!!

Ali ain't fucking around. Ali has reasons for working with Don. Belittling Angelo cuts across all that. Danger's in the air. Dundee puts his hands up.

ALI *(Cont'd)*
You think you're callin' these shots, Don? You're not.

Ali pulls out a comb and starts to comb his hair.

ALI *(Cont'd)*
(to King)
They know!
(segues into a routine)
All those ladies out there know.

Ali being mercurial is unexpected by Don. Laughter from particularly the women as he combs his hair and segues...

ALI *(Cont'd)*
(mock demagoguery)
They know I'm ready! I see fear in the eyes of his followers! I see fear! This is the fight that Muhammad Ali was supposed to be ended. The myth of Muhammad was supposed to fall!
(hits the table with his fist; glares at King)
Supposed to be my destruction!
(French voices and laughter; understated)
They miscalculated. They misjudged. They got it...wrong.

Ali's served notice to everyone with ears to hear it: he's multidimensional, strategic and dangerous as hell. A taste of what's to come.

EXT. VERANDA – ALI, BUNDINI, BINGHAM + ANGELO – DAY

Waiters scurry. Ali talks to a blonde reporter from France and settles next to Lloyd Price, without a shirt. Everyone crowds around their table. A ZAIRIAN INTERPRETER and Lieutenant Nsakala are present. Ali disregards their presence because his attention tracks...

ALI'S POV: VERONICA

seen over the heads of Zairians. She's 5 feet 10 inches tall. Without acknowledging she's the object of Ali's attention, her radar tells her she's the object of Ali's attention.

ALI (V.O.)
Say, girl...!

Veronica turns, sees Ali. Lights up.

ALI (Cont'd)
C'mere. I know you?

OVER VERONICA as she makes her way to the table by Ali's side, where he takes her hand in his.

VERONICA
I don't think so.

ALI
What's your name?

VERONICA
Veronica Porche.

ALI
Like the sports car.

VERONICA
(laughs)
Yes.

ALI
But with a little something extra.
(beat)
Veronica, I know you now. C'mere, sit down.

He steers her into the chair next to him, which is immediately vacated by Lloyd Price.

ALI (Cont'd)
You with Don?

VERONICA
Don brought me here, but I'm not "with"... anybody.

The others are paying them no attention. Bundini stands to talk to Howard Cosell. There's an ocean of side conversations. Ali's presentation to Veronica is natural, open admiring. It is not seduction. It's more seductive than seduction. She feels from Ali nothing predatory or exploitative... only the warm rays of the sun from his open face and appreciating eyes. Still holding her hand...

ALI
Where you from?

Meanwhile, George Foreman, with Sadler, Moore, Broadus, sees and laughs at Ali and Veronica and onto George Foreman going into hotel.

VERONICA
L.A. But my people are from Louisiana. We're Creole. So I'm African, French, Spanish, my mother's grandfather was Jewish.

ALI
(looking at her admiringly)
Well...they all came together real nice.

VERONICA
You know...
(hesitating; low)
...I'm glad you said what you did. You made sure this fight stays here.

ALI
All them writers in there think Foreman gonna...kill me!
(eyes go wide)
What you think?

VERONICA
Ali, boma ye.

Meanwhile, 15 Chinese and some Vietnamese approach and wait patiently. Ali has to force his attention away from Veronica to respond...They all bow. He bows.

The Zairian Interpreter translates English to French to another Zairian, who speaks Mandarin. It all gets lost in chaos while Bingham shoots pictures and a Plimpton type explains pedantically to Bundini...

PLIMPTON TYPE
...she's an African "succubus." Means witch doctor.

BUNDINI
Succubus? Suck my dick. They ain't room in Africa for more than one witch doctor. And that's B'dini.

The eyes of some of the Asians are very emotional. Ali stands up and bows to them. Chinese bow themselves away. Ruth Pointer arrives. Ali kisses her. She sits, but talks to Bingham.

ALI
You been to Hong Kong? Taiwan? Thailand?

VERONICA
No.

ALI
I can't go there. All the ladies out there from Indonesia, Japan, Hawaii, India...
(high-pitched voice, imitating female fans)
"Ali-i-i-e-e-e! Ali-e-e-e! Oh, Muhammad Al-i-i-i!"
(speaks in faux foreign language, imitating female fans; to Bingham)
You seen those people from Thailand? I was in Bangkok — I couldn't walk.
(laughter; hangs his head)
I couldn't...I just couldn't do nothin'. "Get me outta this country!"
(laughter)
The women were so pretty...

BINGHAM
'B-b-b-bout Hong Kong, man?! You know what I heard?

ALI
(interrupts)
Ladies in Thailand, their hair comes down to their knees...and they about Veronica's complexion...and they bad! But they ain't nothin' like the "sisters."
(holds Veronica's hands, looks deep into her eyes)
Ain't NOTHIN' like the sisters!

Veronica laughs as Ali mocks swooning over her...Another news crew arrives.

NEWS CAMERAMAN
Champ...

ALI
(to Veronica)
Let's go for a ride.

EXT. KINSHASA SHANTYTOWN – KIDS – DUSK INTO NIGHT

and old people, teenagers in dirty T-shirts with strange hats. Their eyes are wide.

REVERSE: ALI

shows his bare hands. Now he rubs them together and MAGICALLY pulls from his closed fist a colored scarf. The kids scream.

VERONICA

squints, trying to figure out how he did it, because...

ALI

shows the scarf, pushes back his cuffs so that he can't hide anything up his sleeves. His wrists are bare. He shows both sides. Now, he takes the scarf and pushes with his right hand and feeds it into the closed fist of his left. He looks up wide-eyed at everybody. Then, he opens his fingers and the scarf is not there!

ALI + VERONICA

walk, towering over the kids. One girl holds Ali's hand. The others maintain a respectful proximity so that they don't invade the space around Ali.

ALI
So why you glad we still here?

VERONICA
Holdin' this in Africa make people proud. All over the world. They're proud of you. Anybody can fight in Vegas.

ALI
That's one job. I got two...

They pass through cinder-block houses, shipping crates, oil drums for cooking fires, a few car parts.

ALI (Cont'd)
(melodramatic)
...gotta whup George!

VERONICA
Islamic faith help you to that?

ALI
Listen, girl, as a Muslim, I am busted out and failed in the eyes of God. I shoulda discovered Islam at 50! 'Cause I am weak on women. They take my eyes and my heart follow...causing me to be a lovin' husband and a terrible husband...!
(looks down at her, intensely)
...green eyes and cocoa skin...?
(feigns wobbly legs)
...okay, rest of me, let's go!!

Veronica laughs. She brings his hand up to her mouth and kisses it. Hand in hand, a towering man and a towering woman walk away at their ease against the soft sky with their entour-

age of teenagers and kids. On the perimeter, a kid does flips and, then, gets distracted...

INT. N'SELE GYM – SPEED BAG – DAY

A syncopated, obscuring, blurred shape of the bag turned into a percussion instrument by Ali's fast hands trying to get even faster.

ALI
(to himself)
Faster! Faster!

DUNDEE
(shouts)
TIME!

Ali SLAMS a right hook at the bag. It almost explodes. OPTIONAL: Ali takes body hits, tries sliding off head shots.

INT. RING – ALI'S EYES

feints his left and throws a right. It surprises Holmes.

HOLMES
You can't lead a right hand. Not at him!

ALI
Why not?

HOLMES
Too long...to get it there. Man, I mean, to think you could hit him with a right lead...it's insulting... Nobody would lead a right...

Ali sees something beyond the ring. And, now, flicks four ripping left jabs into Holmes and slides sideways as Holmes tries to catch Ali with a right. But Ali changes directions, changes back and now comes over Holmes' right with his own left cross, and a six- or-seven-punch combination. It is Ali dancing and floating. Crowd cheers..."TIME."

BUNDINI

meanwhile, has thrown his arms around Dick Sadler, Foreman's manager. (We realize this is why Ali segued from serious work to snapping his traditional left jab.)

BUNDINI
I got him! Lock him up.

SADLER
(laughs)
Hey, hold up, chump! Make this chump turn me loose.

Sadler's there with his wife and another

couple. Rudy joins, laughing. Bundini turns loose Sadler. Ali and Sadler like each other.

SADLER (Cont'd)
This is my wife, Irene...

Sadler affectionately puts an arm around Ali's neck and reaches up and pretends to hit Ali on top of the head with a fist for Bingham's camera. Ali bites his lower lip and starts wrestling with Sadler, putting him in a headlock. Sadler's arm is around Ali's waist.

ALI
Hey! Look! Look at George Foreman's trainer, feelin' me up on purpose! On the side, to see if I'm in shape!

More laughter. Sadler's beret falls off. Rudy puts it back on.

IRENE
Can I have your autograph?

ALI
Well, you ain't gonna find no fat! Watch out!!

SADLER
(lunges for wife's note pad)
Give me that thing!

BINGHAM
(breaking through)
Muhammad. Give her an Ali button!

The gang laughs.

SADLER
No, you ain't.
(concedes)
All right, give my wife an Ali button.

ALI
She's gotta put it on.

SADLER
Give my wife one.

BINGHAM
Bo'dini, you got Ali buttons?

ALI
"George" buttons is all I got. In my bedroom! All over the bed! Everywhere! To remind me...of all of ya'. All of ya'! Reminds me of all ya'!

Throughout the above he's pretending to jab at Dick, who's laughing and feinting at him. It's raucous. Fond relationships transcend the adversarial roles. They are all of the tribe of boxers. Sadler is a particularly bright and talented man. Meanwhile...

INT. COMPOUND, OTHER SIDE OF THE RING – AN OLDER BRADLEY

accompanied by an American Reporter is nabbed by a French news crew.

ORTF INTERVIEWER
(in French)
Pardon. Vous êtes de l'ambassade des Etats-Unis? Vous avez une prédiction?

ORTF INTERVIEWER
(English translation)
Excuse me. You are from the U.S. Embassy? Do you have a prediction?

BRADLEY
(in French)
(caught; smiles)
Je suis avec l'Agence américaine d'informations. Il ne m'est pas permis d'exprimer mes préférences entre deux citoyens des Etats-Unis.

BRADLEY
(English translation)
(caught; smiles)
I'm with the U.S. Information Agency. I'm not allowed to take favorites among two United States citizens...

He walks away.

EDGE OF THE RING: ANGELO DUNDEE

sits on the apron of the ring. Ali joins him.

ANGELO DUNDEE
(meaning Sadler)
He gone?

ALI
Yeah.

EXT. COMPOUND – SADLER – DAY

leaving, steals a glance at Ali and Dundee. It's adversarial. The camaraderie was not false. Both are true. But being strategic, he is a threat to Ali. George has a first-rate team.

INT. INTERCONTINENTAL, ALI'S SUITE – ALI – DAY

enters with Howard Cosell and Howard Bingham and a two-man news crew.

BELINDA
Hello, Muhammad. Bingham. Mr. Cosell.

HOWARD COSELL
(tight)
Hi...Mrs. Ali.

ALI
When did you get in?

BELINDA
Just now. Muhammad, may I have a word with you, please?

Belinda starts towards the bedroom. Ali looks to Howard and gestures with his hand to get rid of everybody. As the bedroom door closes, Cosell, crew and Bingham can't wait to get out of there.

INT. INTERCONTINENTAL SUITE, BEDROOM – DAY

BELINDA
What is going on?

ALI
You know what's going on.
(it's not the first time)

BELINDA
But I don't have to have it thrown in my face. I don't have to read about it and have people call me up on the phone about it...

ALI
I didn't mean for it to come out...

BELINDA
Oh, hell, Muhammad, you got no discretion. You never did. You humiliate me!

Belinda slams a lamp standing next to her.

BELINDA (Cont'd)
I clean for you. I cook for you. I feel every punch you take.

ALI
I know that.

BELINDA
Then why you got to be visible with women?

ALI
I didn't mean for it to be...

BELINDA
I live with the casual ones.
(gestures to Veronica's clothing)
But this, this...I can't hold it together anymore.

ALI
I don't want to hurt you. It's wrong. You're a good wife to me.

BELINDA
Then why do you disrespect me this way?!

ALI
I respect you. I always respect you.

Belinda pauses. A terrible question occurs to her.

BELINDA
Do you love her?

Ali doesn't answer.

BELINDA (Cont'd)
Do you want to marry her?

ALI
I follow my heart.

BELINDA
"You're following your heart"?
(sarcasm falls away)
That's what you do. No matter what anybody says. Or thinks. Or what it does...
(pause)
And what happens now?

ALI
I fight George.
(after a beat)
I didn't come this far to lose.

BELINDA
Neither of us did.

Ali looks at her a moment. Then he leaves. Silence. Belinda sits on the bed. She looks up. Then she comes apart. She rips open a closet. She finds Veronica's clothes, rips them, shreds peignoirs, overturns a night table, strips the bed, smashes more furniture, throws Veronica's suitcase at the mirror. It does not break. She looks around the wrecked room. Bingham is standing there.

BINGHAM
Belinda?

Belinda looks up, tears in her eyes.

BINGHAM (Cont'd)
You can't beat him. You can't beat him, 'cause you can't not love him.

INT. ALI'S HOUSE, N'SELE, SHOWER – ALI – NIGHT

under the water. It flows like silver down the contours of his face and neck. He is in that zone of concentration where the best athletes go...where the pre-motor cortex's activity dominates and facial expression becomes

blank, eyes look distantly...Ali's in his domain...in the groove.

EXT. COMPOUND, N'SELE, REAR SHOT: ALI'S CITROEN – NIGHT

and outriders depart.

INT. MOBUTU'S PALACE, A SITTING ROOM – SERVANTS – NIGHT

prepare a luxurious setting. On a platform is a large TV set. In front of it, with low tables are two large armchairs with antimacassars. At the door are Mobutu's spit-and-polish paratrooper bodyguards. They STOMP their feet to attention as...

MOBUTU

in his tan uniform and signature leopard-skin hat enters, followed by an entourage of aides.

> **MOBUTU'S MILITARY AIDE**
> (in French)
> We are ready, your excellent President for Life...

> **MOBUTU**
> (in French)
> Invite Monsieur Idi to join me now...The Banker? The American?

> **MOBUTU'S MILITARY AIDE**
> (in French)
> They are waiting in the sitting room.

INT. ALI'S DRESSING ROOM – DUNDEE

wrapping Ali's hands, tears the tape into narrow strips to go between the fingers. Doc Broadus, from Foreman's camp, observes the wrapping, then signs it. In addition to function, the taping feels ritualistic.

CLOSE: ALI'S

attention is focused elsewhere...on his action: what he will do, his strategy.

> **LIEUTENANT NSAKALA**
> (from doorway)
> Countdown! Countdown!

> **RUDY**
> Countdown is on, bro. Five minutes.

Ali gets off the training table. Angelo has finished. He puts on his robe and starts warming up before the mirror, throwing punches for a full minute.

HERBERT

enters. Ali and Herbert go to an alcove.

> **ALI**
> Thanks to Allah...
> (praying)

> **LIEUTENANT NSAKALA**
> (shouts)
> Four minutes!

Sarria sticking sealed bottles filled with honey, orange juice and water into the water bucket. As Ali puts on the robe, the others gather up the gear, start out. Herbert moves to Ali, preparing for the entrance, to be as close to him for the cameras as possible...

> **ANGELO DUNDEE**
> Give us a moment. Alone.
> (off Herbert's look)
> Hey. This is my religion!

Herbert and Pat Patterson, the bodyguard, with his chrome-plated .45, follow the others away from Ali. Angelo begins applying Vaseline on Ali's face. They're alone in the room.

> **ANGELO DUNDEE** (Cont'd)
> It's hot. Humid. Monsoon season's about to start. May hit 140 in the ring under the lights. You all right?

> **ALI**
> Why?

> **ANGELO DUNDEE**
> Where you at?

> **ALI**
> (looks up)
> Foreman ain't no mummy. He's knocked out eight out of eleven before the end of the third round. He the most dangerous fighter I ever fought.

> **ANGELO DUNDEE**
> I'd worry if I was hearin' anything else.

Ali loosens up his neck.

> **ALI**
> And I can't WAIT!

> **LIEUTENANT NSAKALA**
> Three minutes!

> **ANGELO DUNDEE**
> Dance. That's the most important...

Ali looks at Dundee enigmatically. Before Angelo can ask...

> **BUNDINI**

throws towels across Ali's shoulders.

Ali puts on his long African robe, which is white with African-graphic trim on the cuffs of the sleeves and the hem.

> **BUNDINI**
> (whispers)
> Forget every battle of man against man, of mind against mind, of soul against soul. This is the one. This is the greatest.

Ali nods to him.

> **BUNDINI** (Cont'd)
> This is it.

> **LIEUTENANT NSAKALA**
> Two minutes!

> **BUNDINI**
> The prophet's come back to claim his own! Get the pretender off that throne!

> **BUNDINI/ALI**
> Rumble, young man, rumble! It's the "Rumble in the Jungle"!

WIDE FROM ABOVE: ALI'S CAMP

starts moving towards the door. They open the door. It is guarded by a handpicked squad of paratroopers and Lieutenant Nsakala.

> **LIEUTENANT NSAKALA**
> (shouts)
> One minute!

INT. CORRIDOR

Paratroopers on either side like a wedge, guarding Ali with Angelo, Bundini, Rudy and Herbert, as they push through the door, out into the hall.

TRAVEL WITH THEM AS

people in the corridor at the end see Ali. The chant begins...

> **THE PEOPLE**
> Ali! Ali! Boma ye, Ali! Ali! Boma ye!

The sound from the corridor picks up a second reverberation that booms from a distant vast space. As we move towards it, to encounter it. And suddenly we...

BURST OUT INTO THE STADIUM...

EXT. KINSHASA ARENA – WIDE: EVERYTHING – NIGHT

Lights flood it. They pour down artificial sunshine.

THE PEOPLE
Ali, boma ye! Ali, boma ye!
Ali, boma ye!

ROARS from 65,000 voices at a quarter to four in the morning. The moon is out, revealing storm clouds.

HIGH + WIDE SHOTS: ALI

and entourage. The crowd goes nuts.

TRAVELING WITH ALI THROUGH THE MASS

The crowd roars; Angelo behind, Bundini on one side, Pacheco and Sarria.

EXT. RING - WE ENTER

They cheer. Ali raises his hand and salutes them. Ali dances from one end of the ring to the other...dances into George's corner...The crowd roars.

ANOTHER ANGLE: ALI

dances back to his corner...

ANGELO DUNDEE
George is playing prima donna. He wants to make you wait.

Ali laughs. You won't psyche out Muhammad Ali with that stuff. Instead, Ali uses the time. He tests the ropes. He gets the feel of the distance between the center and the corner.

CLOSER: ALI

circles the ring. He looks at the crowd from different angles, from the corner, the center...He looks up at the lights and gets used to the heat from them.

ALI'S FEET

do a shuffle. He feels the canvas. He feels the soft spots. The firm spots. He feels how much slide there is because of the resin on the canvas, how much spring there is in the boards...

ALI

sheds his robe, now, and throws a blistering array of jabs and hooks. The crowd goes nuts. Ali looks ringside and sees...

ALI'S POV: JIM BROWN

Lloyd Price...further along...Robert Lipsyte.

EXT. ARENA - AISLE - SUDDENLY

out comes Foreman in his red robe, Archie Moore following in his blue pea-cap, and Dick Sadler—never a fashion plate—in the world's least-

attractive T-shirt, followed by former featherweight champ Sandy Saddler.

CROWD
Foreman! Foreman! Foreman! Foreman!

THE RING - ALI

is shadowboxing as Foreman climbs in the ring and crosses past him, near to him. The look on Ali's face is indifferent. Foreman goes immediately to his stool. He doesn't move around the ring. He doesn't touch the ropes.

DISSOLVE TO:

DON KING

as tall as only three other men: Foreman, Ali and Bundini, walks into the ring wearing black...

ZACK CLAYTON,

the referee, moves to the center of the ring. A great roar fills the air: "ALI, BOMA YE! ALI, BOMA YE!"... another one. "FOREMAN! FOREMAN!"

OVERHEAD

as Ali, Foreman and both their crews meet in the center of the ring.

CLAYTON
Now, both of you know the rules. When I step back, I want a good, clean break.
(Clayton keeps going)
No hitting below the belt, no kidney punches, no...

ALI
Motherfucker, you 'bout to discover you ain't nothin'.

CLAYTON
Ali, be quiet!

George's eyes glare. Ali rocks back and forth, ready to rumble.

CLAYTON *(Cont'd)*
No kidney punches. Now...

ALI
(past the ref; eyeballing George)
You been hearin' about me for years. All your life you been hearin' about Muhammad Ali. Now you gotta face me.

CLAYTON
Ali, I'll disqualify you. Now, I want a good, clean, sportsman fight...

ALI
(to Foreman)
You never should have come to Africa.

Foreman is unfazed by all of this. His cold eyes say "battery and homicide."

CLAYTON
(blows up)
All right!!
(beat)
Now go to your corners and come out fighting when you hear the bell, and may the best man...win...

DISSOLVE TO:

Ali turns his back and continues to shuffle and shadowbox.

DISSOLVE TO:

OVERHEAD: ALI + FOREMAN'S

corners are clear. Ali is facing his corner, praying to Allah. Foreman is bent over at the waist, flexing and releasing the last tension in his huge shoulders, as the bell for ROUND ONE clangs...

THE RING - BOTH

charge out and stop as if they ran into a brick wall five feet from each other. Then Ali dips, throws a left, which George takes on the shoulder...a BIG RIGHT HAND to George's head. The crowd goes nuts. George clinches, picks up Ali and swings him through 180 degrees with his power. As he puts Ali down, Ali pushes George's head down and away and Ali clocks him with ANOTHER RIGHT. Foreman clinches and drives Ali back to the rope. Ali throws ANOTHER RIGHT that lands. Ali dances, circles, stays out of Foreman's way. Then he slams him again with a right.

Foreman gets Ali in the corner, throws vicious combinations and a hook that nails Ali in the body and a wild shot hits Ali on the side of the head. CLOSER ON ALI...stunned, his eyes clear. He's just taken a Foreman shot. He pushes Foreman, the stronger man, out of the way and dances and circles. Foreman ties him up again. Ali pushes out, dances and hits HIM with a RIGHT. Ali ties him up, and there's the BELL.

ALI'S CORNER: ALI

ALI
(to himself)
Legs heavy...air's heavy... like sand...

SLOWLY MOVE IN ON ALI

as Angelo and Bundini's talk fades away. We see Ali's awareness in a deep concentration. He is holding counsel with himself. Ali stares into space across the diagonal to the other corner, but not really at Foreman. Ali is weighing something. A gamble. He blinks, and whatever it is, he's decided it NOW. AMBIENT SOUND starts to come back as Ali's attention returns to the present and he ignores...

> **ANGELO DUNDEE**
> ...keep moving. Don't let him put you into the corner. Stay off the rope!

THE BELL FOR ROUND TWO

Ali charges into the center of the ring, provoking Foreman to chase him, and Ali immediately BACKS TO THE ROPE. And stays there! Seizing opportunity, Foreman throws big hooks. ALI IS DOING EXACTLY WHAT HE'S NOT SUPPOSED TO DO. He gets off the rope and backs to the rope on the other side. Most of the shots are blocked by the gloves of both men. No damage. Then George throws a left, which Ali blocks, and a big right hook.

ALI

turns away. Nevertheless, it crashes into his jaw.

MACRO ALI

TIME SLOWS. He ties up George. We SEE Ali's hurt. Dazed. But he must make George believe he's unhurt:

> **ALI**
> That all you got...? That it?

Foreman reacts. Ali takes vicious hooks to the midsection, hangs on and goes right back onto the ropes, tying Foreman up.

LOW ANGLE

George's shots are taken on Ali's elbows and gloves. But for every four that are thrown, one or two tremendous hooks get through to Ali's ribs, his side.

ALI'S FACE

reveals impact, but nothing diminishes the TERRIBLE FORTITUDE with which he endures. Now, he ties up George. Now, George drives Ali into the corner and pummels him.

ANGELO + BUNDINI

going crazy in the corner!

> **ANGELO DUNDEE**
> Get off the ropes! Get off the ropes! Get off the ropes! Dance!

Ali blocking, getting hit. WORRIED FACES in the crowd. One woman looks away.

ALI'S EYES

alive, more than alert, the sharpest eyes in boxing.

FOREMAN'S LEFT JAB

coming in. Ali feints, shifts. It misses by a quarter of an inch.

FOREMAN HOOKS OFF HIS JAB

Ali leans back on the top rope. Foreman's punch falls short and connects with little effect. That's how good is Ali. The techniques BECOME CLEAR.

Foreman goes upstairs, throws three hooks, all get taken on Ali's gloves. Foreman slams a hook that began in Cape Town and ends up in Zaire, into Ali's abdomen. And another. Ali takes the shots, hangs on.

ALI'S EYES

are bright like stars. His white mouth guard shines. A grimace? A grin?

> **ALI**
> (to himself)
> There is nothin'... Nothin'!
> (another Foreman hook lands)
> ...I cannot take.

Ali pushes Foreman off and Ali connects with a left and a straight right to the jaw. They pound but don't stop George. Ali ties him up. Ali's jabs end the round. Nothing effective, but Ali shakes his head, disapprovingly, puts his hand on the back of George's neck, and as the BELL sounds...

> **ALI** (Cont'd)
> Thought you was bad!

George laughs. He won the round overwhelmingly.

ALI'S CORNER

is apoplectic.

> **BUNDINI**
> Dance, dance!

> **DUNDEE**
> Get off the ropes! What are you doin'?!

> **ALI**
> (it gets quiet; to himself:)
> Here come George's "murder" round.
> (refers to Round Three)

Ali pushes away from his handlers and rises. He opens his arms to the crowd. We hear a massive "ALI, BOMA YE" start up.

CLOSER: ALI

opens his arms as if the roar of 65,000 voices is sunlight. By opening his arms, his skin soaks it in and converts it to power. And the BELL STARTS ROUND THREE.

EXT. THE RING

They trade. Nothing. Foreman advances, Ali backs to the ropes, tags Foreman with a couple of harmless left jabs. Now Foreman opens up with heavy artillery. Ali gets in a couple of shots, but for the center of the round he's pummeled by Foreman. Midway through...

FOREMAN accepts a left jab, and while Ali's left arm is out with it, Foreman hammers a right into the exposed lower midsection of Ali and then follows it with six tremendous hooks to Ali's abdomen. Ali pushes him away. Foreman comes in again. Foreman gets him on the rope again, and a surprising right hand explodes on the left side of Ali's face.

ALI

ties up Foreman's left in the crook of his elbow, and they stagger, married, awkwardly, into the center of ring. The referee separates them.

ANOTHER ANGLE: FOREMAN

charging and throwing heavy shots. Ali takes some on his elbows, arms, biceps and shoulders. NOW we see Ali lean BACK. WAY BACK. 45 degrees back...We start to hear the TWANG of the rope. We get it. Ali is using the rope as a shock absorber. Some Foreman punches get through, but the rope TWANGS and Foreman's hitting a trampoline with a hammer. Between deflection and being ring-wise, Ali dilutes much of what George throws. Then Foreman drives three powerful hooks into Ali's side.

ALI'S BODY SPASMS

But, as if inconsequential...

> **ALI**
> George! Show me something.

Ali—insulting, taunting—snaps jabs into George's face, talking through his mouthpiece...

ALI *(Cont'd)*
Where's your punch, man?!

BUNDINI/DUNDEE *(O.S.)*
Ali, get off the ropes! Stick 'em! Jab! Off the ropes!

UP CLOSER: ALI

blocks a rage of Foreman head shots with his fists, the abdominal shots with his elbows. Each Foreman punch is a haymaker.

FOREMAN

suddenly switches.

FROM THE FLOOR: FOREMAN'S UPPERCUT

comes from camera and slams right through Ali's guard, right into his jaw.

ALI'S

hurt! He holds on.

DUNDEE/BUNDINI *(Over)*
Off the ropes! Dance, champ, dance!

Ali's pushed back like a rag doll.

FOREMAN

throws a right hand. It, too, slams through Ali's guard. He's in trouble.

ALI'S EYES

flash. Roll in his head. He sees neon. TIME SLOWS...lights dim...

ALI
(calmly)
...been here before.

ANGELO DUNDEE *(V.O.)*
(distant echoes)
Ali, move!
(beat)
Dance, champ!

Ali glances at the crowd. He SEES: the OLD MAN with the transistor radio on his shoulder from the shantytown, urging him on!

ALI
(to himself)
Open the door, Richard...outta this room...Put on your coat, man...get out...

THE RING: FOREMAN

slams shots into Ali's kidneys, his ribs. Ali will piss blood for two months. But

Ali stays on the ropes. AS TIME CATCHES UP TO NORMAL...

ALI *(Cont'd)*
(to himself)
Think my fight's over...? That...
(to George)
...all you got? That the hardest you hit?

ALI comes off the rope, and Ali hits Foreman with a terrific three-shot combination, a right-left-right. WHAM-WHAM-WHAM. Feints. Hits Foreman with a left-right. WHAM-WHAM!

ALI *(Cont'd)*
C'mon, chump!!!

The BELL. It's an Ali rally at the end. He throws Foreman a look of contempt as he walks to his corner.

ALI'S CORNER

ANGELO DUNDEE
(panicked)
Get off the goddamn ropes!!

ALI
Took somethin' away from him, Angie, that round...

BUNDINI
You gotta move! Stick and MOVE!

ALI
(to himself)
They don't know what's happenin'.

Ali looks to the left and sees Jim Brown.

ALI *(Cont'd)*
(to Jim Brown)
You bet the wrong horse! He can't fight no better than you can act!

Jim Brown laughs.

WE DON'T HEAR A BELL. INSTEAD, WE'RE SUDDENLY IN THE LAST 15 SECONDS OF ROUND FOUR.

EXT. RING, ROUND FOUR, FIVE, SIX – FOREMAN BARRAGE

Ali is braced on the ropes, as far back as the ropes will go. Foreman throws a barrage of shots, he slams in five and six at a time. THE BELL.

ALI

covers with gloves at his head. Elbows at his ribs. When head shots come in, Ali slips them the right or left, or turns them into glancing shots, or just leans straight back so that they all fall short by quarter of an inch. The BELL.

ALI

covering, taking the most powerful hooks Foreman's thrown in the fight, one after the other to the body.

ALI
(to himself)
Take it! Terrify him with what you can take...

Ali's eyes are stars. He sees everything. He sees things no one else can see in the quantum physics of deflecting the force of Foreman's blows.

FOREMAN

desperate, pounds a left to Ali's side, a blocked left to the head, three lefts to the belly, which get through! Ali's left arm convulses downwards, involuntarily, with the blows. What Ali's not ready for and doesn't block is the right hand that follows. This shot is jarring and concussive. He grabs Foreman's neck and has to hold on.

The BELL.

EXT. RING – ALI – MID-ROUND SEVEN

leaning way back at impossible angles—soaking up George's shots. George is SLOWER...BUT Ali's not throwing at all!

ALI
(hisses to George)
Eight more rounds...You runnin' outta gas?

Then...Ali comes out from under.

WHAM. WHAM. WHAM. WHAM. WHAM.

Five hard shots are followed into Foreman's puffed face. They surprise and enrage him.

WIDER: GEORGE

drives Ali with his 220 pounds... George's arms and fists now SWING HEAVILY. Some get through. Ali's right eye is puffy. Both tie up. And BELL ends the round.

EXT. RING – ALI'S CORNER

Angelo and Bundini talk. Neither we nor Ali hear them.

ALI
(to himself to George)
...can't let you get that second wind which you don't know is out there for you.
(talking to George in his head)
Want the title...wear the heavyweight crown?

(to himself)
Jaw broke? Nose smashed?
Face busted in? You ready
to die? Is that you?
(towards George)
'Cause you gonna meet a
man who will die before he
let you win.

A tall African Girl walks by with the number "8." As she passes near Ali, she has the audacity to wink at him. ALI happens to see it. He winks back at her. She smiles. He brightens right up! THE BELL RINGS.

EXT. RING – ALI

goes to the ropes, throws a couple and, now, comes off the ropes. He's in the center of the ring. HE'S HUNTING. A couple of lefts from Ali. Foreman throws a haymaker and almost falls out of the ring. Ali's in the corner, having avoided the shot.

FOREMAN

gets in a couple of lefts that Ali deflects. Ali takes another on the cheek, leans way back again. Suddenly, he seems tired, as is Foreman. Tied up, they go diagonally to the other corner of the ring, both fighters exhausted, leaning against each other. Resting. BUT...

EXTREMELY CLOSE: WE SEE ALI'S EYES ARE DEAD SHARP

He's faking.

FOREMAN

backs Ali into the corner.

ALI

hits Foreman with a left. Foreman launches a short left that Ali counters with a BIG RIGHT CROSS that connects.

FOREMAN'S

head snaps around. Sweat sprays in a parabola of light. Crowd ROARS with expectation. George Foreman tries a right uppercut, fails as Ali circles, guiding Foreman onto the ropes. Foreman's on the ropes NOW.

ALI'S EYES

know the moment is...

ALI
(to himself)
Now...

ALI'S

short, chopping right turns Foreman's head down.

CLOSER: FOREMAN

comes over the ropes and turns back into...

ALI'S RIGHT HOOK

slams his head down and sideways. And Foreman charges into Ali.

CLOSE SLO-MO: ALI

snaps a combination: an overhead right to Foreman's face, a short, chopping left and a right hook. Ali's eyes light up like white phosphorous.

ALI (Cont'd)
(to himself)
RIGHT NOW!

FOREMAN

wrestles Ali to the center. And the most significant moments begin...

SLO-MO: ALI ON THE LEFT + FOREMAN ON THE RIGHT

...and Ali's left hand is extended way behind him with the wrist bent, no power. As it passes his body, Ali converts it into a left hook. As he's doing this, he's dropping his left foot back. The left foot DOES NOT support a left hand. It's for a right hand so the body can untorque across with the punch. And Ali is already cocking his right. Meanwhile, the left connects with Foreman's jaw and raises his chin. As the left is departing Foreman's chin, Ali launches the RIGHT.

SLO-MO: AS ALI'S RIGHT HAND

comes in, Ali's torso untorques, transitioning all 217 pounds to Ali's left foot and putting that weight and power behind his right fist that crashes into George Foreman's chin...and the impact transfers to Foreman's skull...and Foreman's head snaps around. He is gone. He is falling in a spiral...a metaphor for vertigo...turning downward into unconsciousness. And through the spiral, Ali has moved with him, pivoting with the falling Foreman, his right fist cocked to unload again if he has to. He never does...

MASSIVE OVERHEAD: FOREMAN

down. Ali is pushed into the corner by referee Zack Clayton. Foreman is counted out. Clayton raises Ali's hand. 65,000 people go crazy!

TOTAL CHAOS

Ali is seized by Rahaman, Dundee, Bundini. And in the center, hardly seen

by anybody, Ali, now, faints. Veronica, with a DON KING AIDE, is overcome. Tears stream down her face.

EXT. THE ARENA

As if finally released from the suspense, the sky opens. The monsoon begins.

EXT. THE STREETS OF KINSHASA, OUTSIDE THE STADIUM, ZAIRIANS – NIGHT

celebrate. The city is crazy with the air of liberation in the rain. People are drunk, bowing to one another, extending their arms and legs in strange gestures. Laughter. THUNDER is deafening in the downpour. People celebrate despite the storm, dancing on sidewalks on Rua Absini.

EXT. KINSHASA ARENA – NIGHT

Almost empty. The downpour. The last fans rip down one gigantic image of Mobutu...

INT. MOBUTU'S PALACE – THREE MEN

waiting, now rise. One, in Saville Row, is from a London Bank. The other is Bradley, the USIA/CIA character. The third is Idi Amin of Uganda. As everybody shakes hands, they sit down and servants appear. Everyone is pleased with themselves...

BRADLEY
(in French)
Ce soir, le Zaire a été le sujet central dans tous les centres européens. Félicitacions, Monsieur le Président pour la vie.

BRADLEY
(English translation)
Zaire was the center of the world tonight in every banking capital, all over Europe. Congratulations, President for Life.

MOBUTU
Yes.
(then in Lingala to servant)

LONDON BANKER
What's on the menu...?

INT. CITROEN ON KINSHASA ROAD – ALI – NIGHT

rides through the downpour with Belinda and Bingham in the front seat. She gently holds, almost supports his hand.

ALI
(low; about them)
I don't know what's gonna happen.
(beat)
Maan, everything is crazy.

BELINDA
...I didn't come this far to quit.

They drive through a fishing village with dense foliage in part. Ali looks, sees...

ALI'S POV: WOMEN + SOME MEN

have brought their children out into the rain to see the champion so they can say when they grow up they saw him pass by. Plastic or clothing protect the children from the rain. One man holds up his son. Ali rolls down the window.

INT. INTERCONTINENTAL HOTEL, BAR – DICK SADLER

shouting French to the bartender. Folks who look like Jim Brown, Schulberg/Mailer types...hang out, half drunk...and argue about flights out with extortionate petty bureaucrats like Zairian Official #2. Flights have been cancelled, tickets rendered no good, passports confiscated, etc. There's a stoned Hunter Thompson/ Bill Cardoso type with a couple of Zairian hookers. The Hunter Thompson type is not very discreetly smoking Congolese weed.

REVEAL: IN THE BACK CORNER OF THE BAR ARE...

DON KING + HERBERT MUHAMMAD.

King is importuning Herbert, his hands work the air, gesticulating madly, building whole castles of hype and hustle. We can't hear what he's saying. Herbert listens. Then Don King stops and looks at him, and Herbert nods his head "yes." Then Herbert starts saying something and Don King nods his head "yes." Whatever's happening here, a deal for the future has been struck.

EXT. ALI'S COMPOUND, N'SELE – ALI – PRE-DAWN

Rain stopped. The cold, blue light is illuminated with magenta at its base as dawn starts to rise over the Congo River.

WIDE: ALI

in a pale green shirt and slacks, walks towards the water, followed by Zairians, teenagers, some kids who snuck into the compound, two older men. No media; no elite; no hype. One policeman who staggers, drunk. Ali doesn't so much walk to a destination as amble. He rubs the head of a 12-year-old boy who starts shadowboxing five feet in front of him.

ALI
You think you got a chance, chump? Now you in trouble.

Ali begins to spar with the 12-year-old, who is fast and knows a little bit about boxing.

ALI *(Cont'd)*
You even dream of beating me? You better wake up and apologize!

Kid throws a punch. Ali collapses to his knees.

ALI *(Cont'd)*
He too much for me!

Some laughter. Then Ali stands and puts his hand on the boy's shoulder. He ambles with the group towards the river. The sun's coming up on the other side.

FADE TO BLACK.

COLUMBIA PICTURES *Presents*

In Association with Initial Entertainment Group

A Peters Entertainment/Forward Pass Production

In Association with Lee Caplin/Picture Entertainment Corporation
and Overbrook Films

A MICHAEL MANN Film

WILL SMITH as Cassius Clay, Muhammad Ali

JAMIE FOXX as Drew "Bundini" Brown

JON VOIGHT as Howard Cosell

MARIO VAN PEEBLES as Malcolm X

RON SILVER as Angelo Dundee

JEFFREY WRIGHT as Howard Bingham

MYKELTI WILLIAMSON as Don King

JADA PINKETT-SMITH as Sonji Clay

Directed by MICHAEL MANN

Screenplay by STEPHEN J. RIVELE & CHRISTOPHER WILKINSON
and ERIC ROTH & MICHAEL MANN

Story by GREGORY ALLEN HOWARD

Produced by JON PETERS, JAMES LASSITER, PAUL ARDAJI,
MICHAEL MANN, A. KITMAN HO

Executive Producers HOWARD BINGHAM, GRAHAM KING

Director of Photography EMMANUEL LUBEZKI, ASC, A.M.C

Production Designer JOHN MYHRE

Edited by WILLIAM GOLDENBERG, A.C.E.,
STEPHEN RIVKIN, A.C.E, LYNZEE KLINGMAN, A.C.E.

Costume Designer MARLENE STEWART

Music by LISA GERRARD & PIETER BOURKE

Further Reading and Viewing

Books

Muhammad Ali with Richard Durham, *The Greatest: My Own Story* (Random House, 1975)

Howard Bingham and Max Wallace, *Muhammad Ali's Greatest Fight: Cassius Clay vs. the United States of America* (M. Evans and Company, Inc., 2000)

Howard L. Bingham, *Muhammad Ali: A Thirty-Year Journey* (Simon & Schuster, 1993)

Robert Cassidy, *Muhammad Ali: The Greatest of All Time* (Publications International, Ltd., 1999)

Gerald Early, ed., *The Muhammad Ali Reader* (A Rob Weisbach Book, William Morrow & Company 1999)

Thomas Hauser, *Muhammad Ali: His Life and Times* (Simon & Schuster, 1991)

Robert Lipsyte, *Free to Be Muhammad Ali* (Harper & Row, 1977).

Norman Mailer, *The Fight* (Random House, 1975; Vintage Books, 1997)

Mike Marqusee, *Redemption Song: Muhammad Ali and the Spirit of the Sixties* (Verso Books, 2000)

David Remnick, *King of the World: Muhammad Ali and the Rise of an American Hero* (Random House, 1998)

Budd Schulberg, *Loser and Still Champion:Muhammad Ali* (Doubleday & Company, Inc., 1972).

Flip Schulke and Matt Schudel, *Muhammad Ali: The Birth of a Legend: Miami, 1961–1964* (St. Martin's Press, 1999)

Wilfrid Sheed, *Muhammad Ali: A portrait in words and photographs* (Crowell, 1975).

Films

When We Were Kings (1996) PolyGram Filmed Entertainment; a DASFilms presentation; a David Sonenberg production; produced by Leon Gast, David Sonenberg, Taylor Hackford; directed by Leon Gast. Outstanding documentary covers the "Rumble in the Jungle" and related events in Zaire.

The Greatest (1977) Columbia Pictures; a production of British Lion Film Corp. and EMI Films Ltd. Produced by John Marshall; writing credits: Muhammad Ali, Ring Lardner, Jr., Richard Durham, and Herbert Muhammad. Directed by Tom Gries and Monte Hellman. With Muhammad Ali as Himself, Ernest Borgnine as Angelo Dundee, James Earl Jones as Malcolm X, Ali plays himself impressively in this film biography.

A.K.A. Cassius Clay (1970) MGM Corp. and United Artists; William Cayton Productions and Sports of the Century. Produced by William Cayton; directed by Jim Jacobs; written by Bernard Evslin. Stars Ali as Himself, Cus D'Amato and Richard Kiley. Early documentary feature focuses on the controversies around Ali.

Websites

Official *Ali* Site   www.spe.sony.com/movies/ali/
The Sony Pictures Entertainment site allows visitors to view trailers and get all the latest information about the Michael Mann film.

The Ali Center   www.alicenter.org
Information about the soon-to-open Ali Center, a museum and resource center in Ali's hometown of Louisville, Kentucky. The Center's mission is to "preserve and share the legacy and ideals of Muhammad Ali . . . and to inspire adults and children everywhere to be as great as they can be."

HowardBingham.com   www.howardbingham.com
On Bingham's site you can read stories about the noted photographer, view his images of Ali and other subjects, and order his photographic book Muhammad Ali: A Thirty-Year Journey.

Louisville Courier-Journal/Ali page
    www.courier-journal.com/ali/
Ali's hometown newspaper has covered his career from the start, and this site archives more than 30 years of articles and photos. You can also hear the NPR interview with Ali biographer David Remnick and Ali's own recording of his poem "The Legend of Muhammad Ali." Extensive links to other sites.

Muhammad Ali: Float Like a Butterfly
    www.float-like-a butterfly.de/indexe.htm
Well-produced fan site contains bio, photos, pages on Ali's career record and featured bouts, downloadable video clips, fan forum, and links to other Ali resources.

Time 100: Heroes & Icons – Muhammad Ali
www.time.com/time/time100/heroes/profile/ali01.html
Ali's voice greets you and George Plimpton's profile of "The Greatest" anchors Time *Magazine's page on Ali, part of its "Time 100" series on leading figures of the 20th century. Site archives Time, Inc. publications' coverage of Ali.*

New York Times Muhammad Ali page
    www.nytimes.com/books/98/10/25/specials/ali.html
Archives all the New York Times' *coverage of Ali through the decades, including a photo gallery and book reviews.*

Acknowledgments

Newmarket Press wishes to thank the following for their special contributions to this book:

At Forward Pass, the *Ali* production office: Kathy Shea, who kept the book project moving in the midst of a hectic post-production schedule; Morgan Fallon, Sonnet Retman, Susan Hollander, Betty Morin, and Michael Mann's representative, Pat Kingsley.

Mr. Will Smith and his representative, Karen Samfilippo.

At Sony Pictures Entertainment: All those in the various divisions who assisted in the preparation of the book.

At Initial Entertainment Group (IEG): Pamela Pickering, Schuyler Ha.

Unit photographer Frank Connor, for his superb photographs of the production.

Unit publicist and contributing writer Rob Harris, for his insightful coverage of the production, and Electronic Press Kit (EPK) producer Laura Davis.

Book designer Timothy Shaner and Christopher Measom of Night & Day Design; project editor Diana Landau of Parlandau Communications; proofreader Melissa Stein; and Keith Hollaman, Frank DeMaio, Tom Perry, and Kelli Taylor at Newmarket Press.

We are grateful to Howard Bingham, whose long friendship with and wonderful photographs of Ali and his world have added such a rich dimension to our book.

Our deepest thanks go to director and co-screenwriter Michael Mann for his passionate commitment in the making of *Ali* and his generous contribution to this book.

—Esther Margolis, Publisher